Forest School and Outdoor Learning in the Early Years

Forest School and Outdoor Learning in the Early Years

2nd Edition

Sara Knight

Los Angeles | London | New Delhi
Singapore | Washington DC

Los Angeles | London | New Delhi
Singapore | Washington DC

SAGE Publications Ltd
1 Oliver's Yard
55 City Road
London EC1Y 1SP

SAGE Publications Inc.
2455 Teller Road
Thousand Oaks, California 91320

SAGE Publications India Pvt Ltd
B 1/I 1 Mohan Cooperative Industrial Area
Mathura Road
New Delhi 110 044

SAGE Publications Asia-Pacific Pte Ltd
3 Church Street
#10-04 Samsung Hub
Singapore 049483

Commissioning editor: Jude Bowen
Assistant editor: Miriam Davey
Project manager: Jeanette Graham
Production editor: Thea Watson
Copyeditor: Carol Lucas
Proofreader: Isabel Kirkwood
Indexer: Anne Solomito
Marketing manager: Lorna Patkai
Cover design: Wendy Scott
Typeset by: C&M Digitals (P) Ltd, Chennai, India
Printed by CPI Group (UK) Ltd, Croydon, CR0 4YY

First edition published 2009. Reprinted three times in
2009, three times in 2010 and once in 2012.
This second edition published 2013.

Library of Congress Control Number: 2012949087

British Library Cataloguing in Publication data

A catalogue record for this book is available from
the British Library

MIX
Paper from
responsible sources
FSC   FSC® C013604
www.fsc.org

ISBN 978-1-4462-5530-8
ISBN 978-1-4462-5531-5 (pbk)

Contents

Case studies   ix
About the author   x
Acknowledgements   xi
Key for icons   xii

1 Contextualising Forest School   **1**

Introduction   1
Historical roots in the UK   2
From Scandinavia to Somerset   4
Case study: a visit to Denmark   6
The expansion of the Bridgwater idea   8
Case study: the Bishop's Wood Centre   11
Looking forward   13
Discussion points   14
Further reading   14

2 What makes a Forest School?   **15**

Introduction   15
A definition of Forest School   16
Testing the definition of Forest School   21
Case study: a wood on site   22
Case study: a wood within walking distance   25

Case study: a wood that's a short minibus ride away   28
Case study: a special place to go   30
Discussion points   32
Further reading   33

3   Exercise, fresh air and learning   34

Introduction   34
Forest School as a counter to obesity   35
The effects of Forest School on behaviour   37
The impact of Forest School on social development   42
Discussion points   46
Further reading   46

4   Working with parents and carers   47

Introduction   47
Self-esteem, confidence and motivation   49
Social capital   51
Communication   52
Skills, knowledge and understanding   53
Long-term effects   54
Discussion points   54
Further reading   55

5   Seeing the links   56

Introduction   56
Pestalozzi, Froebel and the Steiner philosophy   57
The Montessori approach   58
The Reggio Emilia approach   59
Outdoor Adventure Education movement   60
Te Whariki   60
Building Learning Power   61
Synthesis and development   63
Discussion points   66
Further reading   66

6   Participating in Forest School   67

Introduction   67
Selecting a Forest School site   68
Risk assessment   72

A typical block of Forest School sessions 73
The skills developed during early Forest
  School sessions 86
Discussion points 87
Further reading 88

7 Getting the Forest School ethos into settings 89

Introduction 89
How some aspects of Forest School relate to all
  outdoor play 90
Incorporating the other aspects of Forest School into
  outdoor play 92
Achieving Forest School-type activities in settings 101
Discussion points 105
Further reading 105

**8 Forest School with other groups and
in other countries 106**

Introduction 106
The universal benefits of Forest School 107
Examples in action 108
Case study: Dilham Preschool, Norfolk 109
Case study: Lings Wood, Northamptonshire 109
Case study: Kenninghall Primary School, Norfolk 111
Case study: Essex Wildlife Trust 111
Case study: Green Light Trust Project, Suffolk 112
Case study: Norfolk Broads Authority 114
Case study: SEEVIC College, Essex 114
International developments 115
Conclusion 116
Discussion points 117
Further reading 117

**9 Outcomes from Forest School participation –
some research 118**

Introduction 118
The NEF/FEI studies 119
Storyboarding at Nayland 121
Recording sessions 126
Reflection poster 127

Evaluation of NEF study replication   128
Long-term effects, and whether they are measurable   129
The questionnaires   130
Results   134
New research   138
Discussion points   139
Further reading   139

Appendix: Providers of Forest School training   140
Glossary   142
References and bibliography   146
Index   153

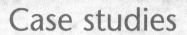

Case studies

This is an indication of where you will find case studies in the book relevant to particular age ranges:

CHAPTER	CASE STUDY (i.e. the topic or title)	AGE RANGE
1	A Visit To Denmark	10 months to 6 years
1	The Bishop's Wood Centre	All ages from toddler to adult trainees
2	A Wood On Site	3 to 5 years
2	A Wood Within Walking Distance	4 to 8 years
2	A Wood That's A Short Minibus Ride Away	3 to 5 years
2	A Special Place To Go	2 to 5 years
8	Dilham Preschool, Norfolk	2 to 4 years
8	Lings Wood, Northamptonshire	Toddler to 5 years plus parents
8	Kenninghall Primary School, Norfolk	4 to 11 years
8	Essex Wildlife Trust	11 to 18 years
8	Green Light Trust Project, Suffolk	11 to 18 years
8	Norfolk Broads Authority	14 to 19 years
8	SEEVIC College, Essex	Students with moderate learning difficulties

About the author

Sara Knight is a Principal Lecturer in early years, education and playwork at Anglia Ruskin University's Chelmsford and Cambridge Campuses. Originally a nursery teacher running a 52-place nursery class, Sara then worked in a special school before moving into the further education (FE) and higher education (HE) sectors. Alongside this, she has been working with the environmental charity the Green Light Trust in Suffolk, running her own Forest School sessions and involved with training in Forest School provision. Sara has written for *Nursery World* and *Child Education* magazines, as well as publishing fiction, both short stories and poetry. Her other SAGE books are *Risk and Adventure in Early Years Outdoor Play* (2011) and *Forest School for All* (2011).

Acknowledgements

My grateful thanks are due to the staff, pupils and parents at Nayland School for their unswerving enthusiasm for Forest School and their assistance in the writing of this book. I would also like to thank my friends and colleagues at the Green Light Trust, at Anglia Ruskin University and at the Colchester Institute, whose encouragement has helped me at every step. Thanks also to the different organisations who have allowed me to refer to their Forest School work in this book: Bishop's Wood Environmental Centre, Bridgwater College, Burthworthy Outdoor Centre, Dilham Preschool, Essex Wildlife Trust, the head teachers and staff of John Bunyan Infants School, Kenninghall Primary School and Lawshall Primary School, Lings Wood Nature Reserve, Norfolk Broads Authority, Norfolk County Council Department of Environmental and Outdoor Learning and SEEVIC College. Last, but by no means least, thanks to my husband David for his patience and his critical eye. David died in 2012, and I miss him every day. I dedicate this second edition to his memory.

Key for icons

Chapter objectives

Case study

Points for discussion

Further reading

Photocopiable

1

Contextualising Forest School

Chapter objectives

- To set the historical context for the development of Forest School in the UK.
- To describe how Forest School started in the UK.
- To contrast the UK setting with an example from Denmark.
- To describe the early development of the Forest School idea in the UK.
- To look towards the future development of Forest School in the UK.

Introduction

This book is for everyone who has heard or seen the expression Forest School and thought 'What is that?' It is also for practitioners who have been on, or are going on, Forest School training courses and want some contextualisation. In addition, it is an attempt to satisfy the curiosity of students and others who are on teaching and child-care courses and have heard about Forest School, and who wish to explore an innovative and exciting way of working outdoors. It is for all who are interested in or are engaged with Forest School, including workers in nurseries and schools, workers in wildlife trusts and ranger services, and students studying for qualifications in these diverse areas. It is more than just an overview, but it is not intended to replace the training process; hands-on experience in the outdoor environment is the only way to acquire a deeper understanding of what it means to be at Forest School.

I have focused on Forest School with children in the Foundation Stage (0–5 years) principally because that is where most of my experience has been, but also because I believe that Forest School can provide a particularly appropriate experience for children in their early years. I have also described some of the interesting work that other Forest School practitioners are carrying out with other groups in *Forest School for All* (Knight, 2011a). Where possible I have used real examples of how Forest School is being put into practice.

Forest School is a way of facilitating learning outdoors, the ethos of which I shall explore in Chapter 2. It is about being in a special place for a minimum of half a day per week and for at least 10 weeks. It resonates with those of us who spent our childhoods either in woods and fields or around an area of streets, messing about with mud and sticks and learning without noticing. Our experiences, too, were about our environment, how to keep ourselves safe, and who we were in relation to the gang of children with us. But before I consider what Forest School is, it is worth taking some time to consider why and how the Forest School movement may have started up in this country. To do that, we need to go back in time and set the scene. This will help us to see where the attitudes and priorities of the Forest School leaders of today have come from.

Historical roots in the UK

Before the urbanisation of the nineteenth century it was not necessary to create formal links between education and the outdoor environment. Children spent large amounts of time outdoors as a part of normal life, and the skills and knowledge acquired there were life skills often related to the food economy or, for the privileged minority, leisure skills (Heywood, 2001: 123, 158). Education was a brief interlude for most, and a source of personal development for the rare few. But when industrialisation caused workers and their families to become crowded into urban tenements which soon became slums, access to the countryside, to fresh air and to healthy exercise became the privilege of the middle and upper classes. Even among these middle- and upper-class families, the move to spend more time in the more crowded cities and large towns curtailed the opportunities for their children to be outdoors. It was this separation of the people from their natural environment, which started in the industrialisation of the nineteenth century, that drew the attention of educationalists and health professionals.

Pioneers such as Froebel and Pestalozzi had pointed out the importance of play in children's development (Pugh, 1996: 93), something that was difficult to achieve in overcrowded slums. In addition, Margaret McMillan and her sister Rachel (Cunningham, 2006: 184; Heywood, 2001: 28) saw what the effects were of a lack of fresh air and freedom of movement, not to mention the poorer diet, on the development of young children and they founded their outdoor nurseries in response. These were largely targeted at children from the poorer sectors of society, recognising the need for access to quality time to play and the need to be in the fresh air for the development of healthy minds and bodies.

At the other end of the social scale there also dawned a recognition that children were not as engaged with their environment as they once had been. In Cambridge, Susan Isaacs's school offered a nursery experience based on the outdoor environment to more privileged children. The Baden-Powell movement at the start of the twentieth century aimed to re-engage initially boys, and two years later girls too, with the outdoor environment; it also required a commitment to contribute to the welfare of others through a wide range of activities from fire-watching in the two world wars to washing cars for charity in the 1960s. Gordonstoun School was founded in 1934 by Dr Kurt Hahn, with the idea of using spartan training methods to develop emotional intelligence and social awareness. In 1941 Hahn launched the Outward Bound movement to address the moral decline of adolescence. So the links between outdoor experiences and healthy minds were recognised at an early date, if sometimes in idiosyncratic ways.

It is my perception that these were often a response to crises in society caused by industrialisation. In our period of history the current crises of obesity, behaviour problems and poor social skills are triggering new responses, and among them is Forest School. It would seem easier to effect change when a crisis can be demonstrated, rather than evolving slowly to avoid crises.

After the Second World War, the 1944 Education Act made access to education compulsory for most children up to the age of 14, rising to 15 in 1947. Eventually, 16 became the universal school leaving age, and what had hitherto been called PT (physical training) became PE (physical education). The PE syllabus included learning about a range of outdoor sports as well as participating in indoor gym sessions. Playtimes were minimally supervised and provided opportunities for rushing about in the fresh air on playing fields as well as on hard surfaces. But in the last quarter of the twentieth century mainstream education in this country seemed to lose sight of the importance of regular outdoor opportunities, with a steady erosion of the time allocated to PE and the sale of playing fields to fund other developments. In addition, a seemingly endless succession of health and safety scares discouraged schools from participating in outdoor activities. This has not happened in other countries, and indeed in Scandinavia and other northern European countries Forest School-type activities have developed as a normal part of their early years provision.

In these other parts of Europe children do not start formal education as early as in the UK (Baldock et al., 2005: 31) and the 2008 interim report from the Primary Review team (Riggall and Sharp, 2008) indicated that they seem to reap benefits socially and emotionally without educational delays occurring. Many countries do, however, provide a range of services for most children below their chosen school starting age, and in Scandinavia these include opportunities that are very like our Forest School (Farstad, 2005: 14). I believe that it is time we reconsidered the needs of preschool children by examining why it is that those northern European countries consider it appropriate to give children time at a key age to develop socially and emotionally without the unnecessary pressure of academic achievement. That the brain of a 5-year-old is 90 per cent of its adult weight (Brierley, 1994: 27) is a strong indicator that the preschool years are important years for development. Maslow's hierarchy of needs illustrated many years ago (1954) that higher-order thinking is much easier when all other conditions have been met (Gross, 1996: 98), including social and emotional security. This book will lend evidence to the argument that Forest School can provide the opportunities for that secure social and emotional development.

From Scandinavia to Somerset

It was a trip to Denmark in 1993 by the early years department at Bridgwater College (see www.bridgwater.ac.uk/forestschool) that started the development of Forest School in this country in the 1990s. What they saw in Denmark were groups of children playing outside in woodland:

> The children set their own agenda, cook [on open fires], listen to storytelling, sing songs and explore at their own level. They are able to climb very high into the trees on rope ladders and swings, and sit and whittle sticks with knives, alone. (Trout, 2004: 16)

This way of working outside with young children was developed in Denmark in the 1950s, but it is not actually called Forest School. In Denmark there are skogsbørnehaven, naturbørnehaven and others. 'Børnehaven' is a translation of the German 'kindergarten', 'skog' means wood or forest, 'natur' is nature and the whole range of provision builds on a Scandinavian tradition of being close to nature. A similar approach is 'Skogsmulle' in Sweden, available to preschool children, and then 'Friluftsliv', which is a part of the national curriculum. Skogsmulle meets daily for three hours:

> The children learn to walk, run, balance, climb, scramble and swing. They also learn about their environment and how to look after it through play, as well as how to respect each other's personal space. (Joyce, 2004: 4)

Norwegian Nature Kindergarten are similar, which is not surprising as 'Friluftsliv' was originally a Norwegian expression, and is entrenched in Norwegian culture. These Scandinavian traditions all adhere to the saying that 'There's no such thing as bad weather, only bad clothing' (Farstad, 2005: 14). As a kindergarten teacher in Norway in the 1970s, I can attest that the culture enshrines contact with and respect for the environment in all weathers. I have been outside at 15 °C with a class of 3- to 6-year-olds, all enjoying playing in the snow because they were dressed appropriately. The correct resources are crucial to the success of any project. We will return to this point in Chapter 7.

Bridgwater College staff and students returned inspired. They began to develop what we now know as Forest School, running Forest School sessions for their own college nursery children. At first they did not have access to a wood, and used the college playing field, but soon found a number of settings within a minibus ride of the college. Having developed a system for early years children, they then offered Forest School sessions to students with special needs at the college, and eventually it became part of the provision for other students in the college. There were benefits to the students' self-esteem, confidence and well-being, which are now being addressed in the Every Child Matters agenda (DfES, 2004), several years before that work was published. How Forest School works with early years groups will be looked at in Chapter 6. This work contributed to Bridgwater College's designation as one of the first Early Centres of Excellence in 1997, and to winning the Queen's Anniversary Prizes Award in 2000.

If you visit Bridgwater College Forest School what you will see and hear about is the transformation of an idea from one culture to another. If you go to visit a Forest School in Scandinavia you will not see a Forest School as we have developed them in the UK, because of the cultural differences from which the two systems have sprung. The concept of early childhood education in Scandinavia is rooted firmly in the philosophies of Froebel with free play, creativity, social-isation and emotional stability at its centre. The cultural norm is of regular access to the environment for the majority of the population, so attitudes to the practicalities of risk-taking, campfires, knives, clothing, and so on are very different from those of the majority of the population in the UK. These factors enable Forest Schools to be more informally integrated into the general early years provision than most UK Forest Schools are currently able to be.

 Case study: a visit to Denmark

I interviewed a colleague on her return from a visit in 2007 to three different early years settings in Denmark. The first was a børne-haven (nursery), taking the usual Danish age range of children, from 10 months to 6 years.

While not wishing to dwell on the indoor provision, it is worth not-ing that there were fewer restrictions from health and safety requirements than are common in most UK nurseries. For example, children of all ages were welcomed into the kitchen area, where they participated in the preparation of snacks and meals, and helped themselves from fruit bowls constantly available. Burning tealights illuminated and cheered the sitting areas, easily within range of the children. There was a woodworking area with sharp and appropriate tools. These are part of the cultural differences that affect attitudes to risk indoors and out.

Outdoors, the baby 'room' was an open barn. Substantial cots with thick insulation provided warm places to rest and sleep in the fresh air. Babies dressed in all-in-one snuggle suits could crawl and toddle freely in the barn and outdoors. They had access to the older children and to their play areas.

The large garden included a firepit for campfires, a large outdoor sandpit (uncovered), trampolines, pets, and areas for car play, domestic play and a sensory area. The divisions were mainly of logs set upright in the ground at varied and interesting heights. A part of the garden had a grassy mound, giving a difference in height, and another had a willow-withy tunnel. The climbing frames were sturdy and adventurous, offering real opportunities to test and develop physical skills. Crates were available as building materials, and frames for weaving. Bird boxes and feeders were located in a quieter corner!

Many of these features are available in our best settings, but it was notable that none of the play resources were made of plastic, and that there were baskets of natural materials available to experience. Also notable was the child-led nature of the play, including on this occasion the collection of berries to mix into mud pies. Adults observed, provided, interacted, but did not dictate. This nursery did not purport to be engaged particularly in the ideals that we associate with Forest School, it merely demonstrated good practice for all early years provision in Denmark.

The second nursery visited was a naturbørnehaven, in other words it offered provision consciously related to the environment. The children were the same age range as above. The resources were also similar, but in addition there was a vegetable garden that everyone participated in tending, and their pets included a goat. The nursery was situated adjacent to woods, and there were daily walks into the wilder areas. In preparation there was a barn containing collecting baskets and places to store wet and warm weather gear. The staff took with them a trolley equipped with magnifiers, identification charts, rope, and so on.

The route through the wood was waymarked, as was the area used in the wood, so that children could find their own way about. In the area of the forest used by the children there was a rope walk, with balancing ropes about half a metre off the ground, and steadying ropes at different heights. There were trees to climb, and children were encouraged to climb as high as they felt safe to do so – quite high in some cases! There were trees to saw, and (it being autumn) a good selection of mushrooms to observe and collect.

The play was again child-led, with the adults as facilitators, providing stimulating additions such as magnifiers, helping children to identify finds and offering support where needed. Children and adults took photographs for recording purposes, and these, together with recording books, create records similar to those used in Reggio Emilia nurseries and the nurseries in New Zealand following the Te Whariki curriculum. (These traditions are explored further in Chapter 5.)

(Continued)

(Continued)

The last nursery, a more extreme naturbørnehaven, was on an island, and the children spent all their time outdoors, with beach, water meadows and forest to choose from. When my colleague and her party visited, the children were building dens to create shelter from the light rain falling. Their firepit burned brightly, creating a focal point and a source of warm drinks. The indoor provision was mostly for displaying and identifying finds and creations. This nursery did not take babies, and there were more boys than girls taking up this opportunity. What it provided was a real adventure for the children who chose to attend, emphasising the importance of choice, and the need for some children to go further and wilder than even the environmentally aware previous examples.

These three examples show how engagement with the environment is a natural and normal part of growing up in all these preschool settings, whether it is a part of their stated agenda or not. The Early Years Foundation Stage curriculum now requires all settings to recognise the importance of outdoor learning for children. This is an ideal opportunity for practitioners to embrace the ideas that come from these other traditions, whether or not they feel ready to engage fully with Forest School.

The expansion of the Bridgwater idea

As might be expected, the Forest School idea has become popular with early years practitioners. Bridgwater College in Somerset developed a suite of courses to transmit the ethos, using Edexcel as their examination board. The Level 3 course soon became established as the standard qualification for practitioners wishing to run Forest School sessions.

There was an early replication of the idea at the Burnworthy Outdoor Education Centre, also in Somerset, where one of the original lecturers from that first trip ran his own Forest School and Outdoor Education Centre. From working with the early years groups, the work at his centre expanded to include work with school refusers, excluded children, women's refuge groups and others. This centre revised and updated the original course, using the Open College Network (OCN) examination board, which has now been passed on to most of the training providers mentioned in the Appendix.

One of the next organisations to recognise the potential importance of Forest School was the Forestry Commission. In 2002 they stated 'access to green space is not just about "the environment". For young children there is perceived to be great benefit in teaching most subjects in a natural environment' (O'Brien and Tabbush, 2002). In 2003 they published regional strategies called Woodland for Life, the vision being 'that trees and woodland are widely recognised as bringing high quality sustainable benefits to all who live and work in . . . [the region's name]' (Render, 2003: 2). On page 47 of this document, the importance of Forest School is recognised (Render, 2003: 47), and the Commission are committed to supporting Forest Schools in the whole of the UK. This was initially done under the umbrella of the Forest Education Initiative (FEI), which deals with the Commission's educational work.

Nowhere has the early support of the Forestry Commission been more marked than in Wales where, together with support from the Welsh Assembly, they funded several successful projects. Forest School leaders in Wales have a strong and supportive network and are developing valuable schemes across the principality. They have further revised the OCN courses for their own use, and for the use of some English groups affiliated to them. One example of the progress they have supported can be seen in the work carried out jointly by the New Economics Foundation (NEF) and the research arm of the Forestry Commission, the Social and Economic Research Group of Forest Research. In 2004 they published the results of a study of three Welsh pilot Forest Schools, *Forest School Evaluation Project: A Study in Wales* (Murray, 2004). This was a first attempt at collecting some information about the effects of Forest School on children in the Foundation Stage. I will return to the subject of measuring, recording and assessing in Chapter 9.

This study was then replicated with a small group of Forest Schools, mostly in the West Country, and published in 2005 as *Such Enthusiasm – a Joy to See; An Evaluation of Forest School in England* (Murray and O'Brien, 2005). In 2006 the findings were put together in a report, *A Marvellous Opportunity for Children to Learn* (O'Brien and Murray, 2006) and the study was replicated in Scotland (Borradaile, 2006), with similar results. This work has been summarised in an academic paper (O'Brien and Murray, 2007), available at http://www.forestry.gov.uk/fr/infd-5z3jvz.

The Forestry Commission supported developments in Scotland, where there are now several Forest School settings, including the two near Fort William used for the report above (Borradaile, 2006). Rangers from the Forestry Commission trained as Forest School leaders and worked with the Forest Education Initiative (FEI) in Lothian. The FEI cluster groups in most Scottish counties, as in many areas in the UK, are re-forming as independent groups following changes in Government Woodland policy.

In 2003 the environmental charity, Green Light Trust, based in Suffolk, was given the task of launching Forest School across the east of England. I led the project, and am proud to see that Forest School in the east is well established, with projects and training taking place in Suffolk, Norfolk, Essex and beyond.

The Green Light Trust is also validated to run OCN courses. I have become convinced that Forest School offers a unique opportunity to children to experience the outdoors in a way that facilitates their holistic development and fosters their growth as confident and competent learners. It also encourages healthy habits and lifestyles (Bond, 2005), a theme I shall return to in subsequent chapters. I have growing concerns that many children were and are being hustled through the most important phase of their education, namely the years from birth to 7, and with an inappropriate emphasis on formal education and conformity to classroom behaviours (see Brierley, 1994: 72). I am not alone in this; other thinkers and writers in early years education internationally are questioning our approach to educating the under 7s (Yelland, 2005). In April 2007 I was a contributor (Bond, 2007) to an international conference called 'Reclaiming Relational Pedagogy in the Early Years' organised by Anglia Ruskin University in Chelmsford. I was thrilled by both the international consensus that young children need time, space and play to develop their fullest potential, and by the reception I received to my proposal that Forest School provided all those opportunities.

Many county councils are now recognising the value of Forest School. For example, Oxfordshire County Council have supported developments from their environmental base at Hill End. Many good ideas have come from the environmental centre at Bishops Wood in Worcestershire, supported by the local education authority (LEA) there (forestschool@worcestershire.gov.uk). Other active county councils include Essex and Norfolk, whose environmental advisers are publishing materials on their websites (see www.schools.norfolk.gov.uk and link to their environmental and outdoor learning team) and wildlife trusts around the country are getting involved in providing opportunities – for an example see www.suffolkwildlife.co.uk and follow the link through education to Forest School. There is a list of training providers in the Appendix, many of whom have websites offering support, advice and links. With the help and support of the Institute for Outdoor Education, 2012 saw the launch of the Forest School Association (FSA), a national governing body for Forest School trainers and practitioners, whose details are also in the Appendix.

 ## Case study: the Bishops Wood Centre

In November 2007 I visited the Bishops Wood Centre to find out about the work that Jenny Doyle had been doing to develop Forest School in Worcestershire. Bishops Wood is an environmental centre run by a partnership of Worcestershire County Council, Worcester College of Technology and the National Grid, and offers courses and support to a much wider range of groups than those engaged in Forest School. However, the work done here to promote the development of Forest School has given it and its Forest School Coordinator, Jenny Doyle, a pre-eminence nationally, creating a good place to visit to gain ideas and inspiration.

Jenny, an experienced nursery nurse, was appointed early in 2000 as Forest School Coordinator, and subsequently moved on to Hill End in Oxford to continue spreading good Forest School practice until she retired in 2012. After completing her own Forest School training she set out to inspire and support all the early years settings in Worcestershire. With 80 acres to work with, Bishop's Wood offers sessions to local nurseries, supported by two Forest School leaders. They provide the children with sets of waterproofs and wellies, and a minibus to collect and deliver the children. Bishop's Wood also runs the OCN Forest School training courses on site, and Worcestershire has trained over 200 leaders in the county. It is not surprising that the centre is an Early Years Development and Childcare Partnership (EYDCP) Early Excellence Centre.

The centre encourages settings who cannot get to Bishop's Wood to run sessions similar to Forest School in their own grounds or in the grounds of adjacent and bigger schools and settings. Part of this support is the provision of a start-up kit for her Level 3 graduates – she has 450 sets of waterproofs, health and safety rucksacks, toolbags, and 'forest baskets' comprising hampers containing mallets, stakes, rope, a camouflage tarpaulin and some collecting buckets. The latter is to encourage leaders to allow for child-led exploration and activity, not to over-organise and dominate the play with an adult agenda.

(Continued)

(Continued)

Figure 1.1   Bishops Wood Forest School, showing one way of storing materials for children to access easily

Apart from the changes that can be seen in the quality of outdoor provision in settings across the county, other benefits have included the involvement of male carers and parents, a group hitherto difficult to engage with the early years settings. In the inner-city areas the Bangladeshi communities have taken to Forest School because of its similarities to the outdoor engagement in their home country, and this has fostered language development opportunities for adults as well as the children. Two men have changed careers and come into early years work. Early years staff from different settings in Worcestershire have seen huge changes in their children, with very quiet children finding their voices as well as energetic children learning self-control.

Other staff at the centre have used Forest School techniques with older groups. A Vocational Inclusion Programme starts with 10 weeks at a Forest School leading to the OCN Level 1 in Forest School. The first group to complete this has gone on to train in green woodwork and building skills using alternative technology. One student progressed on to a Level 2 course and won 'Student of the Year' at the local college. Links now exist with the Top Barn adult training centre, creating learning opportunities in animal husbandry.

A new development is an on-site Danish Garden. A recent visit to Denmark reinforced the idea that more could be done in settings, focusing on the needs of the under-3s, and to this end the centre has constructed an area containing examples of the outdoor items found in a Danish børnehaven. There is the firepit, a storytelling area, and sensory objects hanging and in baskets for sorting. There are willow screens, water features, bird feeders and carvings. There are levels created by constructing a mound in the shape of a sleeping dragon, and a tunnel dugout. This area is for use for training early years practitioners, and for use with groups of children. This is an example of what can be done with creative use of LEA funding. It is to be hoped that over time there will be a greater integration of these ideas into early years practice so that the funding for them becomes the norm rather than the exception.

Looking forward

Individual settings are finding ways to develop their own Forest Schools. For example, I have introduced the idea to Nayland School in Suffolk, where they have a small wood on site (see Case Study on page 22). This is now an established part of their offering, with every child experiencing six weeks of Forest School a term throughout the Foundation Stage and Year 1. Their 2005 Ofsted report also recognised the value of Forest School, said to 'make a magical contribution to children's development' (Goodchild, 2005: 5).

The idea is spreading, and is popular. Many universities are now including teaching about Forest School in their early years and teacher training courses, and the new FSA is providing National Occupational Standards to ensure that the standards are protected and maintained. Reference to the Forest School idea has made an appearance in government reports from both the Department of Health and the Department for Children, Schools and Families as a positive approach to the health and education of young children. As stated above, the Institute for Outdoor Education set up a Special Interest Group which in turn formed the Forest School Association in 2012 as a National Governing Body.

In Chapter 2 we will look at some of the different ways in which Forest School is being offered, and consider what makes a Forest School. With a movement that has spread so far and so fast with little written material to support it, there is a clear danger that the original idea will be lost through lack of understanding. By discussing that unique ethos we can debate whether all the manifestations claiming to be Forest Schools are the genuine article, and thus come to a clearer understanding of what Forest School is.

I mentioned earlier in the chapter my observation that historical changes had come as responses to crises in society caused by industrialisation. As I said, our current crises of obesity, behaviour problems and poor socialisation are triggering new responses, among them Forest School, which has been mentioned in recent government reports (Alexander and Hargreaves, 2007: 13). It is worth looking at these crises, in order to explore the reasons why there is a recognition of the value of Forest School, a story that is not so optimistic or cheerful. In Chapter 3 we will consider the state of children's mental and physical health in the UK, and how Forest School can offer one option as a part of the solution.

 Discussion points

In this chapter I have described the roots of Forest School and its development in this country in recent years. You may wish to find a colleague or colleagues to discuss the following points:

- Forest School could be said to be a response to current crises in UK society. What other responses have there been? Do they, or could they, link into Forest School?
- Forest School is an adaptation of a tradition from Denmark. Are there any other international outdoor traditions we can learn from?
- Action research projects are beginning to build evidence of the short-term benefits of Forest School. What might this mean for early years settings?
- How would you feel about implementing some of the ideas associated with Forest School, such as lighting fires, with the children in your care?
- Some local education authorities are supporting the development of Forest School. What would you see as a possible national model?

Further reading

Bridgwater College Forest School (2001) www.bridgwater.ac.uk/forestschool.
Cunningham, H. (2006) *The Invention of Childhood*. London: BBC Books.
Henderson, B. and Vikander, N. (eds) (2007) *Nature First: Outdoor Life the Friluftsliv Way*. Toronto: Natural Heritage Books.
Maynard, T. (2007a) 'Forest Schools in Great Britain: an initial exploration', *Contemporary Issues in Early Childhood*, 8(4): 320–31.
O'Brien, L. and Murray, R. (2007) 'Forest School and its impacts on young children: case studies in Britain', *Urban Forestry and Urban Greening*, 6: 249–65. Available at: http://www.forestry.gov.uk/fr/infd-5z3jvz.

2

What Makes a Forest School?

Chapter objectives

- A discussion of what turns an outdoor experience into Forest School.
- Four examples of different Forest Schools to test that definition.

Introduction

In this chapter I will start by discussing how to define what a Forest School is, and I will then give four examples from Forest Schools that are already running. This will enable readers to develop an understanding of what makes a Forest School out of an outdoor experience. As you will see below, this is not straightforward, nor is there a complete consensus on the subject. Forest School practitioners are drawn from a wide range of interest groups, including traditional outdoor education, traditional indoor education and different environmental disciplines. Add differing philosophical and psychological approaches to the power of nature, the nature of childhood, and so on, and it is not surprising that there are different strongly held beliefs about what Forest School should be.

This is good. If we are to develop a shared national model for Forest School in the UK there must be robust discussion and debate. It may even be that there is more than one 'right' answer. We also need to consider whether the models developed are sustainable, by which I mean that they can continue operating once the initial excitement and funding have disappeared. From a practical point of view we need to create Forest Schools that will exist over time, not magical events that cannot do so.

In order to help readers through this minefield I have described a range of events called Forest School. The examples are real, and they are currently running. By testing the ethos against the examples given, you will be able to decide what a Forest School is, and whether the models you are looking at are sustainable. All the examples in this chapter are with primary school children in reception classes, to facilitate comparisons.

A definition of Forest School

Debates rage among practitioners about how to express what we know Forest School to be. Each 'knows' at an emotional level what it is, and because it is so special we each feel very protective of it. It almost seems that to put it into words and try to describe it is to threaten the magic. But it must be done and, to that end, this reviewed ethos, and the principles and criteria below, were arrived at after consultation with the Forest School community by the Forest School Institute for Outdoor Learning Special Interest Group, the Forest School GB Trainers Network and Forest School National Governing Body (NGB) working group in 2011. They were pulled together by Erica Wellings, the Forest School (FS) NGB Development Officer and published in February 2012.

Ethos/Definition

Forest School is an inspirational process, that offers ALL learners regular opportunities to achieve, develop confidence and self-esteem, through hands on learning experiences in a local woodland or natural environment with trees.

Forest School is a specialised approach that sits within and complements the wider context of outdoor and woodland learning.

Principles with criteria for good practice (FS = Forest School)

1 *Forest School is a long term process with frequent and regular sessions in a local natural space, not a one-off visit. Planning, adaptation, observations and reviewing are integral elements.*

   - FS takes place regularly, ideally at least every other week, over an extended period of time, if practicable encompassing the seasons.

   - A FS programme has a structure which is based on the observations and joint work between learners and practitioners. This structure should clearly demonstrate progression of learning.

   - The initial sessions of any programme establish physical and behavioural boundaries as well as making initial observations on which to base future programme development.

2 *Forest School takes place in a woodland or natural wooded environment to support the development of a relationship between the learner and the natural world.*

   - While woodland is the ideal environment for FS, many other sites, some with only a few trees, are able to support good FS practice.

   - The woodland is ideally suited to match the needs of the programme and learners, providing them with the space and environment in which to explore and discover.

   - A FS programme constantly monitors its ecological impact and works within a sustainable site management plan agreed between the landowner/manager and the practitioner and the learners.

   - FS aims to foster a relationship with nature through regular personal experiences in a local woodland/wooded site to help develop long term environmentally sustainable attitudes and practices in staff, learners and the wider community.

   - FS uses the natural resources for inspiration, to enable ideas and encourage intrinsic motivation.

3 *Forest School aims to promote the holistic development of all those involved, fostering resilient, confident, independent and creative learners.*

   - Where appropriate the FS leader will aim to link experiences at FS to home, work and/or school/education.

   - FS programmes aim to develop, where appropriate, the physical, social, cognitive, linguistic, emotional, social and spiritual aspects of the learner.

4 *Forest School offers learners the opportunity to take supported risks appropriate to the environment and themselves.*

   - FS opportunities are designed to build on an individual's innate motivation, positive attitudes and/or interests.

   - FS uses tools and fires only where deemed appropriate to the learners, and is dependent on completion of a baseline risk assessment.

   - Any FS experience follows a Risk/Benefit process managed jointly by the practitioner and learner that is tailored to the developmental stage of the learner.

5 *Forest School is run by qualified Forest School Practitioners who continuously develop their professional practice.*

- FS is led by qualified Forest School Practitioners, who are required to hold a minimum of an equivalent Level 3 qualification.

- There is a high practitioner/adults to learner ratio.

- Practitioners and adults regularly helping at Forest School are subject to relevant checks into their suitability to have prolonged contact with children, young people and vulnerable people.

- Practitioners need to hold an up-to-date first aid qualification which includes paediatric and outdoor elements.

- FS is backed by relevant working documents which contain all the relevant policies and procedures required for running FS and establish the roles and responsibilities of staff and volunteers.

- The FS leader is a reflective practitioner and sees themselves as a learner too.

6 *Forest School uses a range of learner-centred processes to create a community for development and learning.*

- A learner-centred pedagogical approach is employed that is responsive to the needs and interests of the learners.

- Play and choice are an integral part of the FS learning process and play is recognised as vital to learning and development at FS.

- FS provides a stimulus for all learning preferences and dispositions.

- Reflective practice is a feature of each session to ensure learners and practitioners can understand their achievements, develop emotional intelligence and plan for the future.

- Practitioner observation is an important element of FS pedagogy. Observations are used to 'scaffold' and tailor learning and development at FS.

- The practitioner models the pedagogy which they promote during their programmes through careful planning, appropriate dialogue and relationship building.

I have developed my own description of Forest School, which would seem to me to be summed up by these key elements:

1 **The setting is not the usual one**. Whether it is actually in a wood, which is the ideal (there is something elemental and magical about a piece of woodland), or in another outdoor area, it is defined as Forest School because it is where Forest School rules apply, not those of the setting that the children have come from.

2 **The Forest School is made as safe as is reasonably possible, in order to facilitate children's risk-taking**. This enables them to learn to respect the environment and move around comfortably within it while keeping themselves safe. In our litigious

society this is the only way to create the freedom to explore and experiment that the children deserve. Forest School leaders are trained to risk-assess rigorously. Once all this has been done, and the paperwork stored as evidence, the sessions themselves can be open and free without fear of reprisal. But it is a 'safe enough' environment, not risk free:

> It is important that children learn to assess and take manageable risks . . . Children need challenge and excitement. If their play environment is made too safe and sanitised, the children will either slump into uninspired and repetitive play or they will find some way to spice up their play environment. (Lindon, 2011: 46)

3 **Forest School happens over time**. When training as practitioners, participants record blocks of six weeks, one half-day each week, but often the best play and the most significant changes are only just starting at this point. Most experienced Forest School leaders recommend blocks of no less than ten weeks, particularly if this is going to be the children's only chance to experience Forest School. Children who are given longer opportunities to participate in Forest School sessions exhibit play that is progressively deeper and more meaningful, and the benefits can be felt when they are back in their usual environments. It is like creating a pathway across a field. The first walker only dents the grass. Only by subsequent feet treading the same path will the path become permanently established. Once it has been established, then even if it falls out of use, the faint trace of its existence will be visible to archaeologists hundreds of years in the future.

This is an analogy for the process of forming neural pathways in the brain and their subsequent myelinisation. The activity of participating in Forest School sessions forms or reinforces neural pathways in the brain. Ways of behaving, communicating and interacting, and the enjoyment of exercise and being in the environment, are reinforced by enjoyable repetition. In the same way, the Forest School experience differs from other forms of outdoor education in that its principal goal is to permanently change the participants for the good, not just to impart a one-off set of information or experiences. To do this takes time.

4 **There is no such thing as bad weather, only bad clothing**. The only time that it is unsafe to go into a wood is in high winds, when branches may break off and fall without warning. That is a time to find an open space, not to go back indoors.

5 **Trust is central**. The adults trust the children to follow the Forest School rules, and vice versa. If you are a leader, you do not go out until you are sure that all the children and adults have understood this. For example, most Forest Schools involve campfires at some point. It is impossible to do this safely if trust has not been gained.

6 **The learning is play based and, as far as possible, child initiated and child led**. There are no time constraints, and risk-taking is facilitated. Forest School is about an internal process of holistic development; something that is difficult to achieve in a busy classroom, indoors or out. Isaacs described play as 'supremely the activity which brings him psychic equilibrium in the early years' (Isaacs, in Bennett et al., 1997: 3). She recognised the need for children to have time and space for making their own choices and expressing their creative spirit. Her focus on open-ended play is also the focus for Pat Broadhead: 'Open-ended play promotes cooperative play, with its higher cognitive challenge for interacting peers' (Broadhead, 2004: 82). This is at the heart of Forest School and its function, which I believe is to connect children – with themselves, with each other and with their environment.

7 **The blocks and the sessions have beginnings and ends**. Because Forest School is such a powerful emotional experience, the children need to be prepared for the block of sessions by the Forest School leader, and to have a significant final session. This may be a celebration with parents invited in, or a campfire with special food, or some other agreed event. Each session has its rituals at the beginning and end to signal the difference and the specialness of Forest School.

8 **The staff are trained**. The sessions are run by a trained Forest School leader, that is, someone who has gone through one of the extensive Level 3 courses delivered by the providers listed in the Appendix. They are assisted by other suitably trained staff and others to ensure a ratio appropriate to the setting and the children.

During the time that I have been actively involved with leading Forest School sessions, or training and observing others doing so, my conviction that it is a powerful and useful tool has grown rather than diminished. I have seen so many children gain from the experience that it is my deepest wish that we could find ways to offer it to as many children as possible. Being in a Forest School with the support and nurture of committed adults creates an unrivalled learning opportunity. For Foundation Stage children it exactly addresses their developmental needs, fostering skills that then help them to succeed in our conventional learning environments (Williams-Siegfredsen, 2005: 26). It also supports the emotional needs of older children whom the system has failed, but that is another story (see Chapter 8).

Taking part in a Forest School session will quickly convince any participant/observer that relationships are a key part of the experience; relationships between children and the environment certainly, but also between each other and between the adults in the wood with them. It is fascinating for me to watch the adults as well as the children, to see who takes to this mode of delivery. It is not for every adult; some of us have outgrown our love of mud and sticks, and it would be foolish not to admit it if it is not your thing – once you have tried it! But there are people who take to this way of working as naturally as the children. They are not all teachers. For example, out of a cohort of 20 trainees at the Green Light Trust in 2007–08, there were 12 teachers, four early years practitioners, one wildlife ranger, and three teaching assistants.

Testing the definition of Forest School

It is helpful to look at some examples of Forest Schools that are being run. By comparing them with the definition described above we can see that Forest School is a flexible approach allowing for differences, provided that the key elements remain in place. I have chosen examples of Forest Schools for children in school settings, so that I can compare like with like. I will use nursery examples in subsequent chapters. At the end of each case study you need to ask yourself whether you would call what is happening 'Forest School' and why/why not. Additionally, you need to consider whether the model is sustainable. If, as I assert, Forest School is a powerful tool achieving great things for children in the early years, then the models of delivery that are developed need to be sustainable over time, and not be dependent upon the vagaries of one-off funds and a single person's excitement.

Case study: a wood on site

Nayland School on the Suffolk–Essex border is fortunate enough to own a small wood that runs along one side of its site. It is separate from the children's normal playing and working areas, but is only a short walk across the playing field from the Foundation Stage classrooms. They have been running Forest School sessions in the wood for six weeks of every term since 2003. Each child in the early years class and reception class attends. In the summer term of 2007 the Year 1 class was also included. The school council has requested that all the children in the school should be entitled to Forest School but before the school can organise this there will be site degradation issues to consider, and it may have to find an alternative site for the older children. Is it Forest School? I shall work through the key elements explained above, and see how Nayland supports them.

1 **The setting is not the usual one**. At Nayland the Foundation Stage classes share a lovely outdoor playground, fenced and safe, used as a part of their normal teaching area. This is not their Forest School. Attached to the school site is a small wood. Other than Forest School, it is only used for an annual Easter egg hunt, and some curriculum-based environmental work with older children. When the children go in there they know that different rules apply, and they do not appear to find it confusing to switch between the different regimes.

2 **The Forest School is made as safe as is reasonably possible**. The Foundation Stage teachers carry out a thorough risk assessment termly, checking the state of the trees and shrubs. The

Figure 2.1   The wood at Nayland School can look wild and different although sited adjacent to the school playing field

main paths are kept clear by them, and the county maintenance staff carry out any arboriculture work necessary. Briars, nettles and fungi are left, and the children are shown how to keep themselves safe. At the start of each termly block of sessions the children and staff negotiate a 'base camp' area delineated by orange plastic tape tied onto twigs. In this area children are free to roam, but need to take an adult with them if they wish to go further. On the days of Forest School the teachers go into the wood at 8 a.m. and undertake a sweep for litter and alien objects.

3 **Forest School happens over time**. Nayland School offers Forest School for six weeks of every term in the Foundation Stage. This can be up to a year in the early years class, and a full year in the reception class. This means that, unless children join the school later, each child will experience a minimum of six and a maximum of 36 weeks of Forest School.

4 **There is no such thing as bad weather, only bad clothing**. I am not aware of any week that has been missed since I launched the Nayland Forest School in 2003. Parents are given plenty of information about their children's needs on Forest School, and the vast majority are enthusiastic supporters. One parent in one class did keep her child at home for two weeks when she felt it was too cold, despite the child's protestations. The Foundation Stage classes have collected a good supply of extra clothing and wellies, so that any child who is ill equipped can be helped to be comfortable.

5 **Trust is central**. When I started the first Forest School sessions at Nayland I spent two or three weeks teaching the staff and children the safety games and procedures. At the end of six weeks it was safe to light a campfire. Since then there has always been an overlap of children between one block of sessions and the next, so they have helped the staff to establish the norms of behaviour, and so on. That is, until the summer term of 2007, when the early years class were completely new. The teacher reported that it had felt strange returning to the basics, but that she had copied what I had done and it had worked. Certainly, by the time I visited in week five the atmosphere was the usual warm and supportive one.

6 **The learning is play based and, as far as possible, child initiated and child led**. There are few time constraints, and risk-taking is facilitated. The teachers do plan the sessions, in that they have targets of skills to facilitate through their engagement in the play, and they have activities to suggest if any stimulation is required. But generally the children have agendas of their own to follow, with the adults offering support and ideas as required – through the sensitivity

(Continued)

(Continued)

of the staff interventions. The time constraints are minimal. There is a break for a snack, which is taken together and is sometimes used as a review, and there is an end to the session, warnings being given 10 minutes before that time is reached. The risk-taking opportunities are not as great as they would be in a wilder wood, but there are poisonous plants to be aware of, and undergrowth that can sting or scratch, as well as logs to balance on and move around.

7 **The blocks and the sessions have beginnings and ends.** The blocks are well prepared for, via discussions with the children and their parents. There is a strong use of photographs, both digitally stored and (for past blocks) made into books to share. Block preparation discussions centre around previous block books. Session plenaries and preparation may involve looking at the photographs taken of that block projected onto the whiteboard. Additional discussions occur as children prepare to go out, and often involve adding verses to their Forest School song to sum up the day's work on their return.

8 **The staff are trained.** The leading staff are senior teachers with many years of experience and a reputation for quality. However, the Forest Education Initiative website (www.foresteducation.org) states that:

In order to run recognised Forest School sessions it is important to undertake the necessary training. Forest School leaders should have a Level 3 qualification. (FEI website, accessed 2007)

This emphasis on the need for training runs throughout the UK Forest School movement, and will undoubtedly be a part of the Quality Assurance schemes proposed by the Institute for Outdoor Learning and by the Forestry Commission. There are three members of the Nayland Staff with a Level 1 Forest School Skills award, which is a familiarisation course lasting two days. It covers the ethos of Forest School, risk assessment and enough practical skills to carry out Forest School-type activities in teachers' own settings. The assessment involves keeping a logbook of the exercises carried out during the course. The Forest Education Initiative website states that the Level 1 award is suitable for 'people who only want to work on existing school/nursery/playwork sites'.

There is also the issue of recognising intuitive Forest School talent. There are particular individuals who respond to the style of play and the environment of the wood in a way that supports and inspires children, without formal training. The staff at Nayland have the intuitive skills to enhance their practice, as well as their formal qualifications. But however talented, even the intuitive Forest School practitioner needs to be aware of health and safety in our society today.

Is Nayland School running a Forest School? Is it a sustainable model?

 Case study: a wood within walking distance

All Saints Primary School, Lawshall, is deep in rural Suffolk. The schoolchildren can walk out of the back of their playing field, along two field boundaries, and arrive within 10 minutes at an ancient hazel wood designated as a Site of Special Scientific Interest (SSSI). Luckily, the owners are happy for the children to use the wood for their Forest School sessions, and the school has a storage shed there in which to keep the essentials. They first experienced Forest School with me in the summer of 2004, and again with Green Light Trust colleagues in 2005 and 2006, but due to staff changes at the school a regular pattern did not emerge until 2007. Now the head teacher is a qualified Level 3 practitioner and uses the cover she provides for each member of staff to take every child in the school into the wood for Forest School sessions, supported by teaching assistants and parent volunteers. Is it Forest School? Again I shall work through the key elements explained above.

1 **The setting is not the usual one**. Frithy Wood is an area of woodland that is privately owned. Local people can walk or ride horses, although few do so as it is away from any roads. The school has the landowners' permission to use this special space free of charge for their Forest School. It is an SSSI because the hazel trees are part of the ancient woodland that once covered much of England, and they were regularly coppiced by the local villagers until the early part of the twentieth century. Since then it has been preserved and cared for. It is not the children's usual setting.

2 **The Forest School is made as safe as is reasonably possible.** The head teacher carries out a thorough risk assessment each term, checking the state of the trees in the area used as a base camp. On her Forest School day she carries out a daily check. The local community woodland volunteers carry out any arboriculture work necessary. No other work is deemed necessary or prudent in an SSSI, and due to the remoteness of the site litter is rarely an issue. The school governors have undertaken working parties to keep the footpaths between the school and the wood as accessible as possible. As the site has public access, the children and staff

(Continued)

(Continued)

negotiate and establish a ticker-tape boundary to remind public and children of the working area for Forest School.

3 **Forest School happens over time.** Each class goes into the wood for five weeks of every term, for two hours. This happens every term and every year, so the effects are cumulative. It is a first school, and the children move schools at the end of Year 4, which means that every child joining the school in the reception year could experience approximately 60 Forest School sessions. At the beginning of each term the children are encouraged to think and plan what they would like to do that term. The final session includes a campfire, and children can invite a grown-up to come and share the session.

4 **There is no such thing as bad weather, only bad clothing.** As before, parents are given plenty of information about their children's needs when on Forest School, and the vast majority are enthusiastic supporters. The greatest issue to deal with has been in the summer months. In 2004 the summer was lovely, and on warm days the children were initially sent in short sleeves and shorts or skirts. The dense leaf canopy meant that the wood was several degrees colder than the surrounding fields, and children complained of feeling cold. Additionally, they were exposed to scratches, grazes and ticks in a way that would not

Figure 2.2 Frithy Wood near Lawshall School with the coppiced stools so useful for materials and for imaginative play

have happened had they been covered up. We learned from that experience, and the range of collected spare clothing has expanded, as has the brief to parents. As Forest School day is Wednesday this has become a non-uniform day for the whole school, which helps remind parents and children.

5 **Trust is central.** The Level 3 training has equipped the head teacher with the necessary safety games to prepare children for the wood. They all know her well in her other persona as their head teacher, who also takes them for art and PSHE (Personal, Social and Health Education) sessions, and as someone with an open-door policy for children and staff. Her children have been pupils at the school, so some children know her as a mum as well. There has been no need to build up the other layers of trust that would be needed were she to be a leader unknown to the children. As the Forest School movement expands, hopefully more staff from different settings will follow this model, and train and provide Forest School for their children, either with colleagues from their setting or in partnership with agencies who can offer complementary expertise. This will help the normalisation of the Forest School experience.

6 **The learning is play based and, as far as possible, child initiated and child led.** The shed contains discovery boxes equipped with the resources needed for particular activities. They have picture labels as well as text, and are designed for self-service. A discovery rug has an activity on it for those children who are not ready to self-start that day. If it is a new activity it will become a box for the following week. A 'guardian totem stick' is given to two children each week to be 'guardians of the forest'. Their job is complementary to that of the system of 'positive play leaders' in the school setting. They help to monitor play, and to ensure that resources end up back in the boxes they came from. This system has to be introduced to new children, so the youngest children are guided into the ways of the Forest School, with the adults facilitating rather than teaching. The older children are encouraged to keep a reflective diary of their Forest School sessions, and to participate in planning the best use of the sessions in advance. The school uses the Social and Emotional Aspects of Learning (SEAL) programme, a government initiative providing resources to schools for monitoring and developing children's well-being, and Forest School sessions include hanging weatherproof faces on the shed door to denote how children are feeling when they arrive. This helps the adults to know where support may be needed that week.

(Continued)

(Continued)

7 **The blocks and the sessions have beginnings and ends.**
   Although the sessions are child led and play based, planning for
   each term is encouraged, so that children use their time wisely.
   At the end of each term there is a celebratory campfire to which
   adults may be invited by the children, but that is the children's
   choice – inviting the adults to share their world for a while.

8 **The staff are trained.** The head teacher who leads the sessions has a Level 3 Forest School award. She is assisted by her
   higher-level teaching assistant, who has a Forest School Level 1
   award, and by parents and others who have not had any training
   in Forest School, but rely on her leadership. Only the head
   teacher has the outdoor first aid qualification. The village
   includes the headquarters of the Green Light Trust, and other
   Forest School practitioners drop in occasionally, as friends of the
   school.

Is All Saints School providing Forest School? Is it sustainable over
time?

 ## Case study: a wood that's a short minibus ride away

Braintree is a growing town, and John Bunyan Infant School is located
on an estate originally of council housing, now with a mixture of
social housing and privately owned homes. Since 2006 the school has
been working with the Daws Hall Centre, an Essex County Council
Outdoor Centre, to offer Forest School to their younger children. The
site they use, Parkhall Wood, is over 4 miles from the school, the last
mile being on private road and track across farmland. They secured
funding from a Woodland Improvement Grant to train staff, and to
provide sets of waterproofs for the children. Does this model conform
to the Forest School ethos? I will describe what I have seen.

1 **The setting is not the usual one.** Parkhall Wood is privately
   owned, like Frithy Wood above. The wood is managed, with staff
   cutting timber and clearing undergrowth. The landowners have
   given permission to the Daws Hall staff to use the wood with
   local schools, although only one school at a time! It is not the
   children's usual setting, and parents have been excited by the
   opportunity offered for their children to have a truly rural experience. As stated, the journey is 4 miles each way. At the moment
   this is accomplished by hiring the community minibus, a cost
   that the school has to bear.

2 **The Forest School is made as safe as is reasonably possible.** The Daws Hall team carry out a daily check. They work with the landowners to ensure the suitability of the sections of wood used at any time. The team has worked with the children to teach them the '1, 2, 3 where are you?' game that all Forest Schools seem to use to prevent children from getting lost (see Chapter 6 for an explanation of the game). At the beginning of each term children are reminded of the safety rules before they leave the school for the first time that term. On the walk from the minibus to the base camp they have 'waiting trees', where the front runners wait for the slowcoaches to catch up. Sticks can be played with, provided they are 'no longer than your arm'.

3 **Forest School happens over time.** In 2006–07 one of the two reception classes went every other week for the whole year. In 2007–08 both have gone every week for the whole year. The head teacher would like to extend this to Year 1 as she has seen significant changes – the Foundation Stage profile went up from 26 per cent to 58 per cent of children achieving 78 points or more after their first year of Forest School, attributable in part to that Forest School experience (there were other factors as well). The class that went in 2006–07 have bonded as a team, an effect that has carried through into Key Stage 1, and they are distinguishable from the class that did not go in this respect. The parents whose children have been are more engaged with the school family, have something to talk to staff about and something they feel they can contribute to.

4 **There is no such thing as bad weather, only bad clothing.** The head was concerned that her catchment area was so diverse that there might be issues with clothing, which is why she bid for funding for waterproofs. These did not arrive in time, but the parents were so convinced of the benefits of Forest School that every child was equipped with suitable clothing on the day. The classes have amassed a stock of boots and warm layers, however, to supplement when children forget a layer. Parents are supportive of the 'there is no such thing as bad weather, only bad clothing' slogan.

5 **Trust is central.** Three members of staff from the school go with the children, so they are with familiar faces. The Daws Hall staff come to the school for a session with the children in their space before they lead them into the woods. Parents are aware of who is caring for their children.

6 **The learning is play based and, as far as possible, child initiated and child led.** I was not able to observe a session, but I am assured that this is the case. Staff are training in a way that encourages this dimension of the ethos.

(Continued)

(Continued)

7 **The blocks and the sessions have beginnings and ends.** As previously stated, the Daws Hall staff have a special session at the beginning of each year, and the staff refresh the children's memories at the beginning of each term. The individual sessions are prepared for and discussed in class time, giving opportunities for reflection and discussion.

8 **The staff are trained.** The Daws Hall leaders are all trained to Level 3, with support staff trained to Level 1. In the school, one teacher trained in 2007–08 to Level 3, and at the date of writing another was undertaking training at Level 3. This gives a secure understanding of the principles and practice in the team.

Is John Bunyan Infant School attending Forest School? Is it sustainable over time?

 Case study: a special place to go

Norfolk County Council is providing Forest School opportunities for Foundation and Key Stage 1 practitioners, both for the PVI (private, voluntary and independent) and the maintained sector. Sue Falch-Lovesey, the Head of Environmental and Outdoor Learning, is driving forward a scheme to train as many early years practitioners as possible at Level 1, so that they can support a Level 3 practitioner offsite, or can develop Forest-School-type activities in their own setting. Much of the training takes place at Houghton Hall Education Centre in partnership with Norfolk County Council, where settings can also come to take part in Forest School sessions. I will focus on Houghton Hall as one example of a setting that Forest School practitioners can use for Forest School sessions. This is not the only place in Norfolk where Forest School is happening, but it is one example, and is interesting in that Houghton Hall is a privately owned stately home where the landowner, Lord Cholmondley, has given local schools and early years settings use of his woodland and a section of the stable block as a base for storage, indoor teaching and display.

1 **The setting is not the usual one.** Most children do not have access to their own stately home! At Houghton, groups usually have the place to themselves; practitioners even report that the children think they own it. Being so special enhances the deep sense of place experienced by all who attend. The children regard the park and woods as a neutral ground, where different rules

apply. It is also a big enough area for each group to have their own space. This model offers an interesting partnership model for other groups to consider, seeking out privately owned land of this nature where other sites may be scarce.

2 **The Forest School is made as safe as is reasonably possible.** The estate cares for the woodland, undertaking any arboriculture necessary. Each Forest School session with the children, and each training session with practitioners, is run by trained staff who check the area to be used before the children arrive. This has recently resulted in moving the base camp areas to a younger patch of woodland, as some of the older trees were safe enough to walk through but not to spend time under. The estate is happy for trained practitioners to light campfires; however, in dry or slightly windier conditions the teams use Kelly Kettles or a bucket grill, which contain fire within the equipment.

3 **Forest School happens over time.** The Forest School sessions run on this site are organised by schools and nurseries where there is a Level 3 practitioner. Sue is hoping to have at least one Level 3 practitioner in each cluster group of schools and early years providers, supported by a number of Level 1 practitioners. The training is planned through the in-service training (INSET) opportunities programme and in consultation with the early years team. The settings will plan the sessions. As at the date of writing, these seemed to work as a core of six weeks on the Houghton Hall site wrapped around by introductory and concluding sessions at the children's usual settings.

4 **There is no such thing as bad weather, only bad clothing.** Houghton Hall is equipped with multiple sets of waterproof clothing and wellies in a range of sizes, usable by Foundation Stage and Key Stage 1 children using the education centre. There is a drying room there, ensuring that clothing is ready to use and easy to pack away efficiently.

5 **Trust is central.** Following the Norfolk model, the leader of the setting is always there, either as a Level 3 leader or as a Level 1 supporter. Sue encourages the involvement of parents as volunteers, and suggests inviting them to introductory and celebratory sessions. This helps the children to feel that they are supported, even though the setting is very different to their usual one. This helps home–setting relationships and the transference of skills between Forest School, settings and homes.

6 **The learning is play based and, as far as possible, child initiated and child led.** Sue provides the Norfolk Forest Schools

(Continued)

(Continued)

with a considerable amount of documentation linking activities to the national curriculum (www.norfolk.gov.uk/outdoorlearning). She recognises that not all children can self-motivate at all times, and that some staff feel the need for planned sessions, so planning sheets can fulfil both these needs. Staff will also model how to use equipment such as pooters and magnifiers, but it is up to the children what they do with them then. The Level 3 practitioners are all aware of the importance of the play-based, child-led approach, and as confidence grows practitioners step back more, observe and are able to use this information to develop a more personalised learning approach to children's needs.

7 **The blocks and the sessions have beginnings and ends.** As the sessions are organised by individual settings, the exact nature of the starts and finishes is up to them. They are expected to make Week 1 at Houghton an acclimatisation week, and generally aim to cook on their last week at least. Parents are generally encouraged to participate where possible in these two sessions, but most are also keen to support every week.

8 **The staff are trained.** As stated, this is the Norfolk policy. There are borrow-boxes available via the children's centres, cluster training and a monthly newsletter that keeps Forest School practitioners in touch with developments (including further training and skills development). Strategic links with the early years advisory team exist and the programme features in the Children and Young People's Plan as a strategic aim.

Is Houghton Hall Education Centre providing Forest School? Is it sustainable over time?

 Discussion points

In this chapter I have asked you to think about what defines a Forest School, and to consider whether there is one model, or whether there are different modes of delivery that are acceptable. This is something you can discuss with colleagues. The following questions might help:

- What are the strengths of each model?
- What are the weaknesses of each model?
- Are you aware of any other models?
- Do the case studies in Chapter 2 conform to the definition of Forest School that I have used?
- Is that definition sufficient?

Further reading

Butwright, C., Falch-Lovesey, S. and Lord, C. (2007) 'Hopton literacy pilot: using Forest Schools experience as a stimulus for speaking and listening, with a focus on raising achievement in boys' writing using ICT'. Available at: www.norfolk.gov.uk/outdoor learning.

Callaway, G. (2005) *The Early Years Curriculum: A View from Outdoors*. London: David Fulton.

Maynard, T. (2007b) 'Encounters with Forest School and Foucault: a Risky Business?' *Education 3–13*, 35(4): 379–91.

Palmer, S. (2006) *Toxic Childhood*. London: Orion.

3

Exercise, Fresh Air and Learning

Chapter objectives

- To consider Forest School as a counter to obesity.
- To consider the effects of Forest School on behaviour.
- To consider the impact of Forest School on social development.

Introduction

In the previous chapters I have stated that changes in attitudes to early years practice and education policy have often come about in response to crises in society. In this chapter I will look at some issues that I consider to be current crises: first, of obesity, then of behaviour problems and, lastly, of poor social skills. I will consider why Forest School might be an important part of a solution, particularly in the early years. I will be expressing my own views, backed up by research evidence and/or the views of others.

Forest School as a counter to obesity

Without doubt, we have a problem with growing levels of obesity in the UK, and one of the most disturbing elements is the increasing number of obese young children. One in four of our children is obese (DoH, 2006). These children may die at a younger age than the current generation of adults unless this trend can be reversed. As well as the risks of chronic illness, BUPA (2007) cites the psychological consequences of obesity in children as 'including low self-esteem, depression and body dissatisfaction' and an 'increased rate of discrimination'. This links obesity with the causes of behaviour problems and poor socialisation that we will look at later in this chapter.

Obesity has many roots, food being only one of them. BUPA (2007) identifies activity habits as key to weight control, and states that 'the good news is that it is probably easier to change a child's eating and exercise habits than it is to change an adult's'. To turn this around, the habits formed in childhood are likely to be those that will inform lifelong attitudes to exercise. Forming these habits of exercise will be a part of the key to tackling this 'health timebomb' (Waine, 2006). The BMA report *Preventing Childhood Obesity* (2005) clearly identifies the desirability of choice in the style of exercise children undertake 'as not all children want to play competitive or mixed sports'. This is a useful justification for Forest School, as it is offering an alternative source of activity for children, and it is offering fresh air at the same time. It is widely available to all children regardless of (dis)ability or need, and it is also developing habits that will last, namely, those of walking and of engaging with the environment.

The benefits of exercise in reducing obesity have been recognised at a government level. In 2004 the Department of Health stated that 'children's and young people's habits and their attitudes to physical exercise impact on the choices they make later in life' (DoH, 2004). This acknowledgement that the formation of good exercise habits at an early age has a long-lasting effect is an important vindication of extending the availability of all forms of exercise. A later paper also recognised the importance of outdoor play in children's levels of exercise (DOH, 2005). The Department for Children, Schools and Families (DCSF) set targets to increase the amount of sport in schools, and in October 2007 claimed that 86 per cent of pupils were now 'participating in at least two hours of PE and school sport per week'

(DCSF, 2007). This enabled these strategies to be used by settings as a justification for funding Forest School initiatives. Under the new UK administration, settings notionally have greater freedom, but often lack the confidence to exercise that freedom.

A relevant question at this point is 'Why are children taking less exercise than in previous generations?' As stated in Chapter 1, until recently the time spent on PE in schools was being reduced, and such PE time that was left in the curriculum was vulnerable to being sacrificed to other one-off demands on time. Alternatives have been suggested, for example after-school clubs have provided some opportunities, depending on the vagaries of staff interests and parent volunteering patterns. This sends messages to children about how we value exercise. As Louv says:

> Parents, educators, other adults, institutions – the culture itself – may say one thing to children about nature's gifts, but so many of our actions and messages – especially the ones we cannot hear ourselves deliver – are different. And children hear very well. (Louv, 2010: 14)

Other messages surround issues of safety. I was fortunate to be a part of the generation who spent most of my free time outdoors, roaming fields and hedgerows as a part of a gang of mixed-age and mixed-ability children. We learned to watch out for younger and less able children, and to identify the skills and strengths we could emulate and rely on. We learned to keep ourselves safe, and we exercised without knowing that we were extending our skills and stretching our bodies. Today's parents receive messages from various sources that the outdoor world is unsafe. They fear for their children, and often keep them indoors unless they can be supervised by adults. They also work longer hours than our parents did, so their leisure time is curtailed, and the activities that need to be crammed into that precious time are themselves compressed and carefully planned. 'Carefully planned' can include swimming, soft-play centres, organised sports, and so on, but nowhere in that scenario is there space for the child to experiment, to make their own decisions and take chances. They are having exercise done to them, and in discrete chunks, not integrating their exercise as a part of their normal life and as autonomous beings. This throws the onus onto the early years settings and schools, where it is recognised that it is important to make time for children to play outside in a sustained way in order to make those decisions and take those chances to provide such opportunities. Whether this is as it should be is a matter for debate at a societal level.

Forest School can offer exercise in a form that can be accessible to all children and at all levels. For example, all the Forest Schools mentioned in Chapter 2 set out to make their sessions inclusive to children with particular needs. I am unaware of any child having been excluded, and am aware of children who have been included although they are not in the groups normally experiencing Forest School (for example, the child with Down's syndrome becoming a Forest School helper for the younger children). As we will see in Chapter 8, Forest School is beneficial for all. So Forest School can be a positive source of exercise for all children, encouraging them all to enjoy exercise and to incorporate it into their lifestyle. In 2005 the Education Select Committee recognised the value of Forest School in enabling children to take 'a carefully monitored element of risk' (Education Select Committee, in Gill, 2007: 65).

As many Forest School activities are self-initiated they are also self-regulated, and allow children to develop their skills and habits over time and at their own pace. For example, children's balancing skills improve as they repeat and develop their skills through their play. Balancing, flexibility, strength and resilience are all physical skills that develop over time. That time can be provided through Forest School. How that happens will be explored in Chapter 6. Developing those skills encourages children to use their physical skills in their daily lives, and in other sports and activities.

Being outside and enabling children to engage with their environment also encourage habits of exercise that can be sustained. To go outside into wild or semi-wild settings is possible for most families. Importantly, it can be done together, it can be free and, as such, it is sustainable. It is also healthier to be in the fresh air where trees are breathing in carbon dioxide and breathing out oxygen, than to be indoors or in crowded stadia for exercise. Evidence from NEF studies shows that not only do the children develop habits of going outdoors, but also that they encourage their parents to do likewise (O'Brien and Murray, 2006: 44). My own research, reported in Chapter 9, describes children recounting an increase in family activities outdoors as a result of their participation in Forest School. In this way, Forest School can become a part of the anti-obesity campaign for all the population, not just children.

The effects of Forest School on behaviour

There is a general perception that more children are behaving in ways that adults find unacceptable, and from a younger age. Reports in the media about bullying, about violence towards children, the elderly and the vulnerable, and about physical damage perpetrated by young people are frequent. Most often the perpetrators of unwanted behaviour are reported to be boys, but this is not always the case.

It is difficult to determine whether the media reports represent a true rise in these occurrences, or just a rise in the reporting of them, as we live in a society more vulnerable to media manipulation than ever before. I shall try to consider the issues as if they were real, but also to consider what events might fuel the perceptions that they are real. This could give insights into the child's-eye view. It is impossible to debate the issue of unwanted behaviour without considering the social and emotional issues that may be causing either the perception or the behaviour, and I shall do this in the next section of this chapter. In this section I will try to focus on other aspects of the behaviour crisis.

Tim Gill in his book about growing up in a risk-averse society describes 'the shrinking horizons of childhood' (Gill, 2007: 12), and how the freedom and independence of children are being eroded by a range of pressures. These include the health and safety scares (banning conker competitions, for example), the delivery of the National Curriculum, the spread of ICT, and the rules imposed by the managers of open spaces over their use ('No ball games', and so on). Richard Louv describes the 'criminalisation of natural play' in the urban areas of the US (Louv, 2005: 27), where the damming of a stream by children in play caused letters to the local paper. Hugh Cunningham describes modern childhood as 'the story of the relationship between dependency, contributions to the family welfare and rights' (Cunningham, 2006: 221). He goes on to describe how we expect children to contribute in the home in a way that gives them responsibility, but then we take away the rights that should come with responsibility with the anxiety we express for them by curtailing their freedoms and pressuring their learning. Jenny Lindon describes our precautionary approach to public settings like playgrounds (Lindon, 2003: 8) so that all challenge and excitement are removed.

These writers are expressing concerns that are felt by many people about the changing state of childhood in this country, a state that has led to our poor rating by UNICEF in 2007 (21st out of 21 industrialised countries in a survey of child well-being). I believe that these changes are going to have implications for behaviour and for the adult perception of this behaviour, and I will explain why I think this is the case. I will consider health, safety and risk first, then consider restrictions on public spaces and, lastly, comment on the effects of living with the pressures of modern life, a theme that will recur later in the chapters.

The activities that children engage in outdoors are perceived to be riskier than those undertaken indoors. This is open to challenge, as more accidents occur in the home than out of it, although the statistics are difficult to collate (see the RoSPA website, www.rospa.com, for details). However, where public spaces are concerned, fear of legislation has meant that the authorities regulating them restrict the activities permissible. There is evidence (Gill, 2007: 16; Lindon, 2003: 9) that suggests where children feel that their environment offers insufficient challenge they will then seek those challenges elsewhere. These can vary from playing near hazards, such as building sites and railways, to throwing objects at shop windows and running away. Therefore, one cause of unwanted behaviour may stem from children seeking out challenges denied them in sterile playgrounds or over-regulated play settings. Mortlock (2000: 50) describes the human 'instinct for adventure', citing Pringle's claim of a fundamental need for new experiences. He links this to the rise in antisocial behaviour, which he describes as a seeking for excitement and challenge no longer available in legitimate activities. It may also be that one perception of unwanted behaviour may stem from adults, observing children finding these challenges on waste ground or prohibited areas, who believe children should conform to the prescriptions of those areas and activities designated 'for children'.

There are contemporary accounts that in bomb-torn cities in the Second World War children often played on the derelict bomb sites, not with permission but with a certain amount of tolerance. And children have often played where footpaths cross rural rail tracks (as I can testify from my own childhood). I also suspect that many small boys have thrown objects at doors and windows or through letter boxes – such an incident is recalled by Dylan Thomas in *A Child's Christmas in Wales*. What has changed to make these activities more unsafe and more undesirable? Perhaps with the latter it is the numbers of children seeking the thrill of challenges unavailable in overprotected spaces. If more children are prevented from taking legitimised risks, then there will be more of them to cross the boundaries into antisocial behaviour. By categorising these kinds of activities as unsafe, I believe that we are taking away from children the right to learn about dangers. We need to take risks to discover the consequences. Roger Putnam states that 'there can be no progress without risk' (Putman, in Barnes and Sharp, 2004: 1). He claims that progress for an individual child is about learning to assess hazards and to deal with them at a progressively complex level.

Forest School can offer young children the opportunity to take risks, within an outdoor area that has been assessed as being as safe as is reasonable. We will look at how to do this in Chapter 6. It can also affect the attitudes of parents and carers to risk, as reported by Natural England in 2009 in their paper on our changing relationships with nature. Changing public attitudes will give our children better chances to be more aware of hazards and how to take sensible risks in the future. Enabling that to happen could help reduce incidents of unwanted behaviours. It might also reduce the perception of what those unwanted behaviours might be.

To consider restrictions on children's play in public spaces, I have already commented on the demise of some school playing fields. Other public spaces where children may play include parks, but may also include bigger and/or wilder areas, such as those owned by the National Trust and the Forestry Commission. To deal with smaller public spaces first, parks often have play equipment such as swings and slides, and many now include ramps for skateboarding and so on. Gill (2007: ch. 2) charts the changing attitudes to playground safety, from the safety initiatives of the 1970s and 1980s to a more adventurous approach by the Play Safety Forum in the twenty-first century advocating opportunities for risk-taking. However, whatever the strategy is in a park, it is rare that children are given the choices and decision-making opportunities offered by an adventure playground (see below). Trees in parks are rarely for climbing, nor are shrubberies for creating dens. In my view, this curtailing of the adventurous spirit is likely to cause a clash between the aspirations of adults and the desires of children, which can be described as unwanted behaviour. Trees to climb and dens to create are a part of Forest School, and creating space for them to be available will help to defuse the clashes.

Adventure playgrounds – another good idea to arrive from Denmark, this time in the 1940s – provided children with a range of materials (less politely described as junk) with which to construct, destruct and reconstruct their own play environments. They were popular in inner-city areas where children had few other opportunities for decision-making play (Bonel and Lindon, 2000: 4). In the risk-averse atmosphere of the 1980s and 1990s many closed, unable to resist the march of safety surfaces and similar restrictions. While an adventure playground is not a Forest School and, as such, does not link the child with the natural environment, it does provide for adventure, challenge and risk. Adventure playgrounds can make a valuable contribution, particularly in urban areas.

Land belonging to the National Trust and the Forestry Commission can also offer opportunities for adventure, challenge and risk. These sometimes take the form of organised activities such as tree-top trails and mountain biking. Adults seem to feel safer if they can describe the activities taking place, and even prescribe where and when they should happen. In addition, protecting fragile ecosystems can require restrictions to human access. But for children, particularly young children, to truly express their adventurous spirit there must be choices and decisions to make, and time to reflect on these and enjoy (or not) their consequences. This is possible in some of the sites belonging to these organisations, but unfortunately not many are accessible to unaccompanied children, as they are in less accessible parts of the country. It is therefore necessary to change the habits of parents and carers before the needs of their children can be met in this way. However, both the National Trust and the Forestry Commission are supportive of Forest School, providing land and arboricultural support, which extends the choices available to Forest School leaders.

The last part of this section will briefly consider the effects of living with the pressures of modern life, linking this section both with the next and with the previous section. Some will consider that this section contains sweeping statements, but they are my perceptions based on over 20 years of working in the early years sector. Previously I described how the busy lives of parents and carers often mean that leisure time is curtailed by their working lives, but this can also apply to children. The demands of the curriculum and the aspirations of parents may mean that time to contemplate, reflect and relax is more limited than in previous generations. Organised exercise such as Tumble Tots and swimming lessons are all valuable, but if a child's life is organised throughout every day they will never learn to rely on their own resources and develop their own brain skills.

Children's rushed lives combined with a lack of access to the natural world is described in Sue Palmer's book *Toxic Childhood* (2006: 47). This is leading to stress-related conditions and illnesses in progressively younger children, including preschool children. Behaviour problems resulting from such a lifestyle may include poor concentration, motivation and social skills. There are even links described between the rise of attention deficit hyperactivity disorder (ADHD) and the separation from nature (Louv, 2005: 101). Boys are particularly vulnerable to the restrictions and constraints placed on them by modern living. Environmental psychology would say that boys, designed to grow strong enough to tackle a mammoth and establish their position in a tribal society, need space for rough and tumble, and for energetic games. Constrained, and without the early language skills of the majority of girls, the result is a manifestation of the behaviour problems described earlier. As you will see in Chapter 9, research shows how Forest School can help with all of these areas.

Contact with nature has been shown to protect the psychological wellbeing of children (Louv, 2005: 49). This is one reason why most of us feel better after going for a walk or after working in the garden. In the USA there is research evidence from two universities: Texas A & M University has researched the beneficial effects on stress levels of viewing natural scenes, and the University of Minnesota is developing designs for therapeutic gardens. Forest School can help promote positive behaviour by providing for the normal needs of normal children, by addressing the roots of problems in others, and by helping children to develop acceptable coping strategies. By providing Forest School from the beginning of the Foundation Stage, children will have the best opportunity to develop resilience to the pressures and problems described above.

The impact of Forest School on social development

Practitioners in nurseries and schools are reporting that increasing numbers of children have poor social skills. Anecdotally, this would appear to me to be a problem that continues to accelerate as children become older, with greater numbers exhibiting antisocial behaviour. We have discussed some possible reasons for this in the previous section, most of which were at a community level. By looking at trends in families, we can identify further reasons that link to children's development and the conditions in which the foundations of social behaviour are being laid down. It seems that if the foundations are not built properly, then the house will always be at risk of subsidence or collapse. I shall use those aspects of social development listed in the Early Years Foundation Stage Curriculum (DfES, 2007) as a starting point to illustrate possible reasons why children's social skills are not developing as practitioners would wish:

- **Dispositions and attitudes**. This starts with babies developing self-awareness, including influencing and being influenced by others, and sharing experiences. To foster this, the Practical Guidance recommends devoting uninterrupted time to playing with babies. This can be difficult when parents are anxious to return to work, to pay bills or maintain careers, and even the best quality childcare settings cannot always replace the special focus of attention of a loving main carer. Without the consistent care of one or two main carers there is a risk that children will not receive the feedback that they are special, and that their individual differences and preferences are valued. The possibility of negative feedback will feed into the development of motivation and interest in learning about new things and new people.

- **Self-confidence and self-esteem**. The guidance emphasises the importance of feeling safe and secure within healthy relationships, so that children feel able to move from a position of strength to develop confidence in their own abilities. Consistent and loving care which is expressed with warmth is central to this security, and through no one's particular fault, modern children often experience changes of care through staff changes in nurseries, changes of nursery, dislocations in family care, and a general sense of bewilderment rather than security. In addition, in daycare settings children are often separated from siblings because care is arranged in age-related rooms to accommodate different staffing ratios. This insecurity will affect children's abilities to express their needs and feelings appropriately, and to respond sensitively to the needs and feelings of others.

- **Making relationships**. Building from a secure attachment to one or two people, babies and young children develop a capacity first to make relationships with other special people, usually family or carers. As children grow towards school age, their social circle widens, and they learn about adapting behaviours in different settings, and strategies such as waiting and sharing. These important skills are predicated on that early attachment. Previous sections have shown that for many young children that early experience is not as sound and secure as is ideal, and, as a result, attachment may not be secure, and the other skills that should follow will develop shakily on weak foundations.

- **Behaviour and self-control**. Consistent boundaries give children security, and enable them to know what responses to expect from their carers. From that foundation they can develop their understanding of how to respond to others, to other living things and to the environment. This is the beginning of an understanding of right and wrong. Again, consistency depends on continuity and all the carers in a child's world following the same pattern of care. We fail our children if we do not give these clear signals from an early age, and allow our tiredness or stress, or lack of communication between carers, to move those boundaries. We should not then be surprised if older children continue to push boundaries. In part they are seeking to know where 'stop' is, in part they are seeking gratification that they know from experience will come if they are persistent enough.

- **Self-care**. Babies are often keen to begin the self-care process, signalling their discomfort, hunger or thirst, and grabbing the spoon at mealtimes. Young children will want to begin to do things for themselves, to dress themselves for example. These skills develop their abilities around health and hygiene, but also affect their abilities to choose activities and resources, all important learning skills. Of course, learners take longer to do things than experts, and children need time to practise and hone their self-help skills. In our rushed age this has become more difficult, which has contributed to the phenomena of older children who are 'bored'. They are not really bored, they just have not developed the skills to choose and to self-help. They are likely to exhibit unwanted behaviour, because they may know no other way to elicit the attention they need.

- **Sense of community**. Bronfenbrenner (1990, cited in DfES, 2007) described the child's expanding world, developing from a secure base to explore 'similarities and differences that connect them to, and distinguish them from, others' (DfES, 2007). With a positive self-image a child is more likely to treat the cultures and beliefs of others with respect, because they present no threat to them. They already know that their own family's beliefs and culture are respected. Once again, the secure base is the key to future development, and, once again, consistency and time are key elements in constructing that secure base. It will be difficult for the older child to reflect on the needs of others if they have an underlying sense of insecurity about their own needs being met. It will be much easier to lay blame for society's woes at the feet of people who are demonstrably different from ourselves if we feel a general sense of insecurity about who we are and where we belong.

This is just one way of looking at how poor social skills can be endemic in today's children, and how these can then result in unwanted and antisocial behaviour. The causes could possibly seem to be in changing childcare practices without the infrastructure to counter its effects on our youngest children. By this I mean the efforts successive governments made to enable mothers to return to the workplace by encouraging affordable childcare, before realising that we needed a graduate-led workforce to ensure the appropriate quality of care for *all* of our young children. Hopefully, this is beginning to change, but the problems that these policies have created will take at least a generation to work through. The important point is that there is deterioration in children's social skills, and that Forest School can help in the remediation process.

Forest School sessions in the early years have been shown (Murray and O'Brien, 2005) to increase motivation and concentration in children. Confidence and self-esteem are improved as skills develop and no one fails. This has a snowball effect, because as confidence grows so the children find more exciting things to do, which they will succeed at, thus improving their sense of self-esteem even more. A part of the Forest School process is to engage the children in setting the rules and boundaries (see Chapter 6). This makes them easier to stick to, and behaviour improves. The lessons learned in Forest School transfer back into the classrooms and nurseries, improving behaviour there too.

Activities in Forest School are as child led and child initiated as possible. There are some children who, by the age of 4, have lost the ability to spontaneously play outdoors, and therefore there is a place for adult contributions and enhancement but, as much as possible, Forest School is child led and child initiated. This increases children's abilities to choose and to self-help, skills useful in the classroom and beyond. This is particularly important for children with particular needs, who are even more vulnerable to losing control over their own lives. Fi Hopkins is eloquent on this subject in *Forest School for All* (Knight, 2011a: 123). The case studies in Chapter 2 show that Forest School pulls parents, staff and children together, developing concentric circles of communities: the children, the settings they are in, and the local community of parents and friends enveloping the whole. This gives a sense of security and belonging to the children and their parents.

Discussion points

In this chapter I have considered the rise of obesity and the role Forest School can play in fostering good and sustainable habits of exercise for all children. I have discussed the effects of a real or media-fuelled perception of the rise in antisocial behaviour, and some possible causes, together with why Forest School experience might provide a chance to counter this. Lastly, I described the concerns of practitioners about the increasing numbers of children with poor social skills. I have explained my view that these poor skills have their roots in earliest childhood, and described some of the counter-effects recorded when young children experience Forest School. You may wish to discuss these points further. Here are three questions to consider:

- How is your setting helping children to form the habit of exercise in their daily lives?
- How can we enable children to take risks and experience adventure in early years settings?
- What are the strategies you would use to provide babies and toddlers with social and emotional stability?

Further reading

Gill, T. (2007) *No Fear: Growing Up in a Risk Averse Society.* London: Calouste Gulbenkian Foundation.

Louv, R. (2005) *Last Child in the Woods: Saving Our Children from Nature-Deficit Disorder.* New York: Chapel Hill.

Nilsson, K., Sangster, M., Gallis, C., Hartig,T., de Vries, S., Seeland, K. and Schipperijn, J. (eds) (2012) *Forests, Trees and Human Health.* New York: Springer Books.

Waters, J. and Begley, S. (2007) 'Supporting the development of risk-taking behaviours in the early years: an exploratory study,' *Education 3–13*, 35(4): 365–77.

Working with Parents and Carers

Chapter objectives

- To describe some of the ways in which Forest School can be used with parents and carers.
- To explore reasons why this is beneficial.
- To suggest further developments for this thread.

Introduction

When I first visited Burnworthy Outdoor Centre, before beginning my own training as a Forest School leader at the beginning of this century, one project there moved me profoundly. The centre offered Forest School sessions to the local Women's Refuge. In the morning, children and mums worked in separate groups, enabling leaders to respond to their different needs, offering a form of ecotherapy to one and a play-based developmental opportunity to the other. At lunch time they came together and shared food, that archetypal way of bonding, caring and sharing. After lunch they worked in small family groups with a practitioner who modelled ideas for play and behaviour.

In my book *Forest School for All* (2011a) there are two chapters linked to this early encounter. The first is Chapter 14, where two workers in a Sure Start centre, Lucy Partridge and Wendy Taylor, used a Forest School approach to work with family groups, many of whom were struggling to cope for a huge variety of reasons. They found that they could influence family engagement, and thus improve the outcomes for both adults and the children, using Forest School sessions. They suggest its value as a tool for Strategic Planning for Children's Centres, as a cost-effective way of addressing a wide range of family support.

The second is Chapter 13, where Mike Brady describes working with Phoenix Futures to use Forest School with a group of adult addicts, some of whom were parents. One of his case studies, on page 191, describes how Forest School enabled a mother to begin to rebuild her relationship with her 10-year-old son. It also helped her to gain the confidence to change the relationship with her key workers, and thus improve her future prospects.

Looking closer to home, in the third of the case studies in Chapter 2 of this book I describe the Forest School run for the reception classes at John Bunyan Infant School in Braintree, and comment that the catchment includes social housing. The head teacher is a convert to Forest School, and not just because of the beneficial effects on the children. She has also seen the effects on potentially difficult-to-reach parents who feel that in Forest School they have something to offer as volunteers, including fathers who would not normally come to the school. Also, the outdoor sessions seem to be a point of contact between staff and parents/carers, enabling conversations that did not take place when the points of contact were around the formal curriculum.

These four different events can be examined to consider why using Forest School to work with parents has important potential. The rest of this chapter is taken up with a discussion of the key similarities between each of these events, which relate to the outcomes for children already identified by the NEF studies (Murray and O'Brien, 2005), and listed below:

1 **Confidence**. Increased self-confidence and self-belief from freedom, time and space, to learn, grow and demonstrate independence.

2 **Social skills**. Increased awareness of the consequences of their actions on other people, peers and adults, and an increased ability to work cooperatively.

3 **Language and communication**. More sophisticated written and spoken language prompted by children's sensory experiences at Forest School.

4 **Motivation and concentration**. A keenness to participate in exploratory learning and play activities, an ability to focus on specific tasks for extended periods of time.

5 **Physical skills**. Improved stamina and gross motor skills through free and easy movement; improved fine motor skills by making things.

6 **Knowledge and understanding**. Increased respect for the environment, interest in natural surroundings; observational improvements – identify flora and fauna, changing seasons, and so on.

I have adapted these headings so they relate to adult participants, and hope thus to highlight that this is an area ripe for further development. My new list highlights the priority areas for working with potentially vulnerable adults, in a sequence that builds up as the events described above built up:

1 Self-esteem, confidence and motivation.

2 Social capital.

3 Communication.

4 Skills, knowledge and understanding.

Self-esteem, confidence and motivation

Mental health charities such as Mind (Peacock et al., 2007) and academics such as Burls (2007) have written extensively about the importance of our relationship with nature in promoting mental as well as physical health. Observing and reading the reports of the events above support this assertion. In atmospheres freed from stress by the sympathetic support of Forest School practitioners, the adults described above could relax and participate each at their own level, just as the children do. It is not surprising, therefore, that the outcomes are similar.

The women from the refuge, socially excluded by the traumatic events in their lives, found that a connection with nature enabled them to rediscover their sense of who they were and what they could achieve, through tasks as simple as lighting a campfire. Sharing the preparation of a shared meal in a natural environment enables the strengthening of relationships with each other, with the practitioners and with the children. Through this comes self-esteem and confidence. The children experienced the outcomes we have come to expect from Forest School, plus the bonus of seeing their mothers grow in stature and skills.

Lucy and Wendy also reported increases in self-esteem in both children and their carers, ascribing it to the no-fail environment at Forest School. The bonus of having some staff trained both as Forest School practitioners and as early years support workers helped them to create an atmosphere where discreet observations could lead to advice and support, and parents could grow in their sense of self and self-esteem. This also led to adults taking on a more equal partnership with day-care providers, more aware and thus more confident of their role.

The Phoenix Futures group already knew each other, but for them the wood, and being on trust not to resort to their addictions, created a different atmosphere, where nature was there to support and nurture them through their challenges. It became a powerful coping mechanism that needed to be sustained longer than was initially anticipated, but its value in raising the self-esteem of the participants was measurable. Self-esteem is something that has to be recognised by the person themselves, as was the case with this event, which is recorded in Chapter 13 of *Forest School for All* (2011a). This in turn can raise levels of confidence, a powerful aid to the lady in the case study mentioned above.

For John Bunyan Infant School, the parents they most wanted to reach were those least likely to come forward. With either poor experiences of school themselves, or disaffected by later experiences, many parents previously failed to connect with teachers. Through volunteering to help with Forest School, or simply by having the common ground of Forest School for chatting with staff, parents seemed to feel better about themselves and confident that they had something of value to contribute. After all, not all of the staff liked going out in the cold or wet, and not all of them could offer the skills that some of the parents could provide, so the scales were perceived to be more evenly balanced, thereby raising the self-esteem of the parents.

Social capital

Something that all of the groups observed and written about above have in common is that they have lost social capital. By that I mean that the social relationships that have positive benefits for the participants have been reduced by circumstance. Gaining or regaining these for the adults will be as important for the life chances of the children involved, as it will be for themselves, and will be built on the self-esteem and confidence gains described above.

For the women from the refuge, the relationships they were building as a group could help them to move forward, giving them confidence to deal with authority figures in a less passive way. Lechte (1994) identified the importance that post-feminist thinkers place on women as a sisterhood, supporting each other to achieve and succeed. Rather than being rescued and hiding in a refuge, they created a camp where each had a role to play and something to give to the community, and reciprocity was the glue for maintaining the social bonds they were creating. Their children will then be able to see them as they see themselves, as active participants, not victims.

Similarly, the families from the Children's Centre are being encouraged to take the lead in their children's lives. With increased skills which raise confidence, they are partners with the day-care providers, and are forging a network of support with other families attending the sessions. This is almost a 'secret society' of parents and carers who can light fires, create games and have fun together in a wilder space, which can make them feel special and supported.

Potentially, the addicts have lost most of the social capital they had, and such a loss can be more damaging, and more difficult to rebuild, than building from a point that was never very high. Reading the chapter is a lesson in just such rebuilding, first the self-esteem, then the confidence, and through that some sense of agency. It is the belief that they can interact with the wider world, and that they have some self-belief that gives them an appropriate status, and that restores to them some social capital. Without social capital they are unlikely to be able to reclaim children and loved ones, as 'others' with greater capital will make decisions for them but without them, decisions that affect their futures. This is one of the powerful effects of Forest School, that by building confidence we also build a sense of agency and autonomy.

The social capital that parents acquire as a result of the Forest School activity in their children's school is three-fold. It is around the truth that they have something of value to give the school, their time and skills, which raises their capital. It is around the kinship that they build with like-minded parents and staff encountered through the Forest School sessions. Lastly, it is around the improved outcomes for their children, seeing them valued as members of the school community.

Communication

Communication occurs at many levels and in many ways. Starting with communication with external agencies, the sections above indicate how Forest School will enable the participants in the different groups to feel more empowered to engage with the authority figures who enter their lives. Feeling that they are a part of a community can enhance this confidence still further.

An interesting debate that links communication to respect and to spirituality (Moss, 2009) can make us think about being people first in our professional encounters with others. The groups described above will, through their Forest School experiences, be developing their self-respect, and be communicating with their inner selves in natural spaces, which is likely to be a spiritual encounter. The sections above affirm that they will be becoming stronger, but this will still require the acknowledgement of other professionals in their lives to take those new developments forward. Communication between participants, Forest School leaders and the other professional leaders in their lives becomes key.

In all of these groups, key workers participated in the Forest School sessions, becoming led as well as being leaders. This facilitated key workers' appreciation of the journey travelled by the adult groups, and facilitated a different kind of communication between them and people hitherto regarded as clients. Just as teachers and early years workers who join in the Forest School session with their children meet key workers as whole people and learn new things about them, so too do these workers. And as the children learn that these adults are not omnipotent and infallible, and meet them differently in Forest School, so the adults here have an opportunity to meet the workers on a level playing field with the balance of power in different places from where it is outside Forest School.

This seems to be an important element in Forest School, the fact that it can provide a transition to new ways of communicating through mutual respect and the warmth of human interactions.

Skills, knowledge and understanding

Too many adults in the modern world have had too few opportunities to engage with the wild world, and very few in their adult lives. Simon Barnes emphasises the importance of a connection with nature in his book *How to be Wild* (Barnes, 2007). Forest School leaders know the importance of that contact for children. Contact with nature brings respect for the natural world but also respect for its dangers. Climbing trees, using knives and proximity to fire cause dangers, but also give young children an enhanced sense of agency, resourcefulness and responsibility (Blackwell and Pound, 2011). The majority of group members in all four of the events described above were not familiar with wild spaces, and were naturally concerned for the welfare of the children who might be with them in those places. The Forest School leaders were able to model and instruct, and through that process enable the adults to feel more skilled and knowledgeable about the world they inhabit. As a result, they had a new resource for life at their disposal, one that is cheap to access and enjoy.

The skills acquired will vary according to the location of the Forest School and the make-up of the groups, as well as the skills of the Forest School leaders. The Burnworthy group and the Phoenix Futures group benefited from being led by leaders with extensive bushcraft skills and being located in spaces where it was possible to engage in a wide range of activities. The Children's Centre group and the John Bunyan Infant School group were led by leaders with skills appropriate for working with young children in more cultivated spaces, so the skills they could transmit were simpler, based on campfire and craft activities. But even these were able to empower the adults to feel confident to meet nature on her own turf and feel comfortable in that environment.

Waite and Pratt (2012) argue that place will have new meanings and potential as a learning context; the child and others have learnt from interaction with others and then return to the place with developed expectations. Within this model, place plays an active part in the learning activity with which the child engages and in the pedagogies employed. In the case of Forest School, that place is a wooded area that for a number of weeks has been a base camp, enabling those using it to develop a deep connection with nature and its rhythms.

A combination of new skills and time spent in a new place is built on the previously described qualities to enable adults to feel that being outside in a wild space is a positive experience. It is an experience they would wish to repeat and would like to help their children to engage with. The result of increased confidence and some new skills has been observed to be calmer and more connected adults and children.

Long-term effects

Leading on from the previous section are thoughts about the potential long-term impact of using Forest School when working with adults. Some of these can be deduced quickly. Increased social capital and a stronger sense of agency and purpose can affect communications and therefore the potential outcomes for families.

The effects could, however, be even more long-lasting, if we believe writers such as Louv (2010) and Barnes (2007). We need to find the wild in each of us for our own lasting health, but also for the health of the planet: 'Living a wilder life is a better way to live: it has more meaning, it is better for our minds, our hearts, our souls' (Barnes, 2007: 329).

Engaging with young children is a wonderful thing to do, and easy; they want to be at Forest School and have few inhibitions about throwing themselves into everything Forest School can offer. How sustainable the impact is on their lives in the future will also, in part, depend on how we can engage with their parents and carers in the process. The groups I have used to illustrate this chapter are groups of adults with different and sometimes acute needs, but all parents can benefit from the opportunity to engage with Forest School, just as all children can benefit. Then, perhaps, the planet will also benefit.

 Discussion points

As yet, the focus for Forest School is rarely on working with families but, hopefully, I have raised the potential for discussion. All parents and carers can benefit from being involved in Forest School sessions, and many have skills and experiences that they can offer to enhance the children's experiences. These may complement and extend the skills and experiences offered by the Forest School leaders. It is up to individual leaders to manage how to engage parents in the process in positive ways, and it is this process that can exercise settings.

- What could you do to promote a positive relationship between the Forest School leader and the parents?
- How would you introduce the concept of risk benefit to your parents?
- Would you ask parents to support sessions that included their own child, or different ones?
- How would you explain the beneficial outcomes of Forest School to parents?
- Would a guidance booklet be helpful?
- Would any of your staff feel inhibited by the presence of parents at your sessions?

Further reading

Blackwell, S. and Pound, L. (2011) 'Forest Schools in the early years', in L. Miller and L. Pound, *Theories and Approaches to Learning in the Early Years*. London: Sage.

Burls, A. (2007) 'People and green spaces: promoting public health and mental well-being through ecotherapy', *Journal of Public Mental Health*, 6(3): 24–39.

Morrow, V. (2010) '*Children's "social capital"*', in J. Rix, M. Nind, K. Sheehy, K. Simmons and C. Walsh (eds), *Equality, Participation and Inclusion*. 2nd edn. Abingdon: Routledge.

Moss, B. (2009) '*Ethics, vision and values: the challenge of spirituality*', in J. McKimm and K. Phillips (eds), *Leadership and Management in Integrated Services*. Exeter: Learning Matters.

5

Seeing the Links

Chapter objectives

- To consider some historical perspectives on early years care and education that may have affected the development of Forest School.
- To consider contemporary ideas which share some of the characteristics of Forest School.
- To consider what such an overview can tell us about the place of Forest School in the tides of change that move through early years care and education.

Introduction

Forest School does not exist in a vacuum, but in the context of other thoughts and ideas about working with young children. Some pre-date Forest School in their inception, and may have influenced its development, either before or after its importation into this country. I count here the influences of Pestalozzi, Froebel, Steiner, Montessori and Reggio Emilia, along with influences from the Outdoor Adventure Education movement. Others have developed in parallel, such as the Te Whariki curriculum from New Zealand and

Guy Claxton's 'Building Learning Power'. Research undertaken by The Economist Intelligence Unit has compared the outcomes from early years education in different countries, pointing out that 'as countries increasingly compete on the basis of their talent and human capital, they need to invest in all their people as early in life as possible' (Economist Intelligence Unit, 2012: 31).

The revised Early Years Foundation Stage Curriculum (EYFSC) in England came into force in 2012, and while it recognises the importance of the outdoor environment in the development of young children, it has removed the emphasis of the previous Early Years Foundation Stage (EYFS) on access to outdoor environments on a daily basis. The EYFS is not a philosophy, but it does express the approach of the UK government to the care and education of children aged 0–5. I have not dealt with it here, but in Chapters 6 and 7 I do make links to the EYFSC for the benefit of practitioners in England. Other UK curricula (Scotland, Wales and Ireland) do rather better in their overt links to outdoor learning, so I have not dealt with them in the same depth, as the links are clear to see.

By looking for similarities with other approaches and philosophies we can illuminate further the factors that make Forest School an important strand in early years provision. I will briefly discuss each of the above perspectives in approximate chronological order. By the end of this chapter you should know where Forest School sits alongside these ideas, and possibly have some ideas for further synthesis and development.

Pestalozzi, Froebel and the Steiner philosophy

'The Steiner Waldorf approach to education in the early years holds nature, the rhythm of the earth, cycles of life at its core. It is an approach to education where children play without the interference of adults' (Oldfield, 2001). This statement links Steiner to Forest School immediately. Nature- and child-led, it is designed to support the physical and spiritual growth of the child. It is very much based on the philosophies of Froebel (1782–1852) and of Pestalozzi (1746–1827).

Froebel pioneered play as learning, and outdoor play as central to this, not surprising given his two-year apprenticeship as a forester while in his teens. His development of the use of specific objects made of natural materials (gifts) links his work to Montessori. He created the term 'kindergarten', and encouraged children to be in the outdoor environment, and engaged in construction and exploration. He worked with Pestalozzi in Switzerland for a while, and both men pioneered the idea of active and open-ended learning for young children. These philosophies provided the basis for the Steiner movement.

From its roots in Germany in the early twentieth century, the Steiner method of education has spread across the world, offering parents the choice of a system that claims to 'honour and protect' the wonder of childhood. Steiner believed that in the early years imitation and example are more important than words. As in Forest School, the teacher is a provider and a guide, and has responsibility for providing an environment that will stimulate free imitation, awakening the child's will and initiative. Creativity and make-believe are encouraged as young children learn through their senses, and their life experiences and social interactions are very important. There is an emphasis on the environment and on using natural materials, and children are encouraged to take risks outside in their play, just as they are in Forest School. They are also encouraged to experience awe and wonder outside, and domestic sensory experiences indoors, and they call their early years provision 'kinder*garten*' (my emphasis), a term which originated with Froebel and which translates as 'children's garden', again emphasising the links with nature.

It would seem that the Steiner approach to education in the early years is very close in ethos to Forest School, which is no surprise when one considers the northern European links in this early years philosophy and where the origins of Forest School are found. The Scandinavian and German approaches are all largely founded on Steiner principles, and it is from the centre of that geographical region that we have taken the original Forest School idea. Without a doubt Steiner and Forest School are a close fit. The major difference is the inclusion in the Steiner methodology of the domestic and indoor elements.

The Montessori approach

Maria Montessori's work in the slums of Rome in the early twentieth century, devising a curriculum based on formalised tasks, may not seem at first glance to link to Forest School. But through her work she demonstrated the importance of repetition, teaching that children need to repeat the tasks she devised in order to learn the concepts embedded in them. Her work was mainly with children with learning difficulties, but in Forest School we know that all children need the chance to repeat their activities because that is how the neural pathways in the brain are created and mylanised.

Montessori also valued equipment that was made from natural materials, enhancing the sensory experience of her activities. In recognition of the importance of natural materials, many Montessori nurseries are keen to provide outdoor sensory play when children's tasks have been completed. Discussing Forest School with a tutor from Montessori Education (UK), she was of the opinion that had Montessori been alive today she would have embraced Forest School with enthusiasm.

The Reggio Emilia approach

Loris Malaguzzi started his pioneering work in northern Italy, working to repair the damage inflicted by the Second World War on the health and well-being of young children and their families. The Reggio Emilia approach to early years provision, like Forest School, values individuality and personal development, and encourages creativity. The children initiate ideas with the adults facilitating and encouraging the development of the children's learning. Adopting this kind of process allows for the Reggio Emilia 'possibles', the opportunities to explore the multiple dialogues among children. This is a listening and observing approach, such as those which are also used in Forest School.

The Reggio Emilia approach is not centred on outdoor environments, nor on natural materials. The similarities between this and Forest School are in the centrality of the child, and the importance of listening and observing. It is the children's ideas that drive what happens, rather than a prescribed curriculum. In addition, the importance of the community is considered, with high parental involvement. Forest School is compatible with this, but is different, as with the other approaches described.

The other useful aspect to consider about Reggio Emilia is the way in which the children's work is recorded. The practice of taking photographs and finding idiosyncratic ways to record achievements is helpful to Forest School practitioners, who will wish to communicate progress to settings. I will pick up on this theme when I discuss Te Whariki, and again at the end of the chapter.

Outdoor Adventure Education movement

It may seem strange to have this heading as an example of a different perspective in a book devoted to one type of outdoor education, but traditionally Outdoor Adventure Education has been concerned with providing older children and adults with the opportunity to challenge themselves in settings and ways that are extreme for them. These are often one-off opportunities, although enthusiasts will return for more. The one-off nature of the experience is completely different from the Forest School ethos. It relies on the challenge offered to participants being sufficient to create a memory of success that will carry them forward with increased self-esteem for as long as that memory is fresh. Hopefully, by the time the memory has faded, the increased self-esteem has enabled the individual to have achieved sufficiently in their lives for that self-esteem to have become a part of their self-concept. In Forest School the challenges are less extreme, and the change in self-concept happens as a result of the repeated drip of increased self-esteem over time.

Other aspects of Outdoor Adventure Education are similar to Forest School. The fact of the environment being different, hopefully with a sense of wildness, and the importance of cooperation and empathy are the same. Fostering a love and respect for nature are now common aspirations. Colin Mortlock, a famous outdoor educationalist, adventurer and writer, describes feeling 'as if I were part of the ocean environment . . . accepting fully that everything around me was somehow related to, and part of, me. It was the deepest feeling of peace and harmony' (2000: 112).

Importantly, assessing hazards so that participants can take risks are similarities that Outdoor Adventure Education and Forest School share. The risks are different, but the assessment processes should be no less rigorous. Now that Forest School has been a Special Interest Group within the Institute of Outdoor Education, practitioners will be able to access advice and support from Outdoor Adventure educationalists about these issues. As I have repeated frequently throughout the book, this is an important element of Forest School, preparing children to cope with danger and risk in their future lives.

Te Whariki

This curriculum was published for the New Zealand Ministry of Education in 1996, with the aspirations for children 'to grow up as competent and confident learners and communicators, healthy in mind, body and spirit, secure in their sense of belonging and in the knowledge that they make a valued contribution to society' (New Zealand Ministry of Education, 1996: 9). It is illustrated as a woven mat comprising principles, strands and goals, and links to the curriculum framework for schools. The four broad principles at the centre link to the aspirations of Forest School.

The first principle is of empowerment – empowering all children to learn and grow. Forest School has the same inclusive aspiration, based on valuing the individual skills and contribution of each child. The second principle reflects the holistic way children develop. In Forest School we enable children to use every part of themselves to thrive and grow. The third principle is that the wider world of family and community is an integral part of the early childhood curriculum. Reports from Forest School projects show how the children's participation has fostered stronger links between settings, families and communities. The fourth and final principle is about relationships, considering the fact that children learn through responsive and reciprocal relationships with people, places and things. These different relationships are just what Forest School aims to provide. These general principles can be interpreted in many ways. Forest School is one way, Te Whariki another. Some aspects of interpretation are different. For example, an early years practitioner from New Zealand visited a Forest School session with me and loved it, but feared that the health and safety legislation in New Zealand would prevent him from setting up a similar scheme there.

One New Zealand interpretation that could be useful to Forest School is in respect of the recording system used, described by Margaret Carr in her 2001 book, *Assessment in Early Childhood Settings*. This is a system similar to that used in Reggio Emilia and mentioned above, one where the children participate in selecting what is to be recorded and how. In New Zealand these records are called 'learning stories'. Children may take their own photographs, and choose their own pictures and artefacts. Adults listen and observe, and add their own notes. When children move on, their records are made into a learning storybook to share. In this way individuality and personal development are valued, and creativity encouraged.

Building Learning Power

In other chapters I have indicated how comfortably Forest School sits with Guy Claxton's ideas on Building Learning Power (BLP). The skills and aptitudes that this programme is designed to promote are very similar to those encouraged through Forest School, so in a school working to foster these it would be very hard to sort out the effects of BLP from the effects of Forest School over time. With both Forest School and BLP, the programmes move their focus from the 'what' of learning and development to the 'how', working to develop the child's abilities first to cope and then to succeed, rather than measuring the facts that they can regurgitate.

This child-centred approach can withstand the winds of change that regularly blow through our education system and through the world of work beyond. Claxton states that 'to thrive in the twenty-first century, it is not enough to leave school with a clutch of examination certificates. You have to have learnt how to be tenacious and resourceful, imaginative and logical, self-disciplined and self-aware, collaborative and inquisitive' (Claxton, 2002: Introduction). All these skills are developed through Forest School.

As early years workers, we are encouraged to be reflective practitioners. It is strange, therefore, that our curriculum does not place greater emphasis on encouraging children to reflect. In Forest School the time and space that they are given enables that to happen. Again, this links to BLP, 'mulling over experiences, either alone or in discussion with others, looking for useful lessons and generalisations that can be drawn out and articulated, and which can therefore be consciously applied to new situations' (Claxton, 2002: 33). These sound like skills for older children and adults, but I have experienced this happening with 3- and 4-year-olds in Forest School. It is just that mulling and generalising with young children tend to be observed by adults as practical and physical activities.

Of course, BLP is not exclusively an outdoor approach to learning. But children who have had a Forest School experience in the Foundation Stage move seamlessly into this approach. Sitting and reflecting around the campfire translates to sitting and reflecting in the classroom. Cooperation in moving logs prepares the child to work with others, valuing their skills and contributing their own (reciprocity). Using the natural environment helps develop resourcefulness, and feeling good about yourself, increases resilience.

Synthesis and development

Examining other approaches to education enables us to more fully appreciate what it is that we value about Forest School. Coming through strongly from all the examples above is the idea of the child as an individual, developing uniquely with different strengths and talents to be nurtured and valued. In order to facilitate this there is a need to focus on a child-led approach, not a curriculum-driven one. This tension between the activity-based approach to early learning (indoors or out) and the listening-and-observing approach exemplified by Reggio Emilia and Te Whariki demonstrates a difference in paradigms. There are many theorists and practitioners in the early years sector who are embracing the paradigm shift from starting with a curriculum to starting with a child's interests and concerns. This theoretical shift is embraced by writers, thinkers and practitioners who are described as post-structuralist or post-modernist.

One member of staff participating in Forest School sessions with the children from her setting told me that through Forest School she was able to get to know her children more closely. She was seeing the whole child, with their unique talents, rather than spending her time looking and measuring levels of skills and knowledge. This sad indictment of the Foundation Stage curriculum lends evidence to the arguments of the post-structuralists, some of whom say 'in short, the idea of curriculum is too normative, ordered and confined to live alongside the complexity, unpredictability and respect for difference that define a "pedagogy of listening"' (Dahlberg and Moss, 2005: 106). Alongside a pedagogy of listening is the idea, voiced by Claxton, that we are not preparing children for work in the twenty-first century.

Our education systems were designed for an industrial society. We no longer have that societal structure, and therefore the skills and talents we require from our putative workforce are very different. Ken Robinson claims that creativity is the key to success in the modern world and that, currently, our curriculum suppresses rather than encourages it: 'New curricula must be evolved which are more permeable and which encourage a better balance between generative thinking and critical thinking in all modes of understanding' (Robinson, 2001: 200). In Forest School, children use natural 'found' materials to express their natural creativity in many different ways. They make music and dance, they create stories and visual images, one example of which can be seen in Figure 5.1.

Figure 5.1 An abstract sculpture of found objects arranged by 4-year-old children in independent play

The creativity expressed above does not exist in Forest School alone, but plays back into the rest of the children's lives. Ken Robinson states:

- Human intelligence is essentially creative. We not only find meaning in the world, we interpret it through structures of ideas and beliefs. We each create the world we live in.

- We do this through the power of representation – of symbolic thought. We experience the world in many ways and use different ways to make sense of it: including words, images, sounds, movements, gestures and many more.

- Our ideas interact with events and are capable of profound change. If events can be construed, they can be misconstrued and reconstrued. (Robinson, 2001: 112)

If fostering creativity is central to a child-centred approach to supporting learning and development in the early years, then Forest School is a good example of how to go about it. Forest School can be seen as a manifestation of the way in which some theorists are rethinking how we should be encouraging children to learn. It is about creating confident, communicative and creative children who can make the most of their potential. No one who has experienced Forest School denies the powerfulness of the experience.

Changing one part of our approach to supporting learning and development will inevitably mean other changes. If we are going to recognise that we are dealing with a different paradigm, we also need to embrace a different recording system, one that also starts with the child rather than the curriculum. In the sections above I described how Reggio Emilia and Te Whariki settings use a learning story approach, creating something like the sketchbooks suggested by Gill Robinson in her 1995 book *Sketchbooks: Explore and Store*. During the Forest School sessions in Chapter 6, the teachers and the children took both moving and still digital images of their activities. This is not unusual at Forest School, and links well with the idea of building learning stories, and is a start to that process.

In the Chapter 6 sessions, any associated literacy work was carried out after the Forest School time, with the children using the experiences of the morning to experiment with ways of telling other people about their experiences, using ICT and more conventional writing skills in combination. This illustrates that already the Forest School experience can be complementary to the children's learning in conventional school, giving time and space for experimentation, consolidation and reflection. The recording process also needs to be reflective and consolidatory in nature. Clark et al. (2003) identify how rarely children are consulted about their own education, still less about their own educational success. Forest School, with its child-led ethos, can help to change that. I believe that we should be creating sketchbooks or scrapbooks that contain not only photographs, but also snippets of conversation and comments, artefacts (or photographs of these) – in fact anything that seems of importance at the time to anyone engaged in the process, adult or child, to create a resource for reflection back in the classroom. Teachers could then extract such information as is needed for assessment, and children could use them to 'hold the moment' and reflect on their experiences in a rich and meaningful way, as happens in New Zealand. In this way the different skills, talents and interests of the children can be encapsulated and rewarded in a wide and holistic manner. 'A single endproduct is not always sufficient evidence of the thought processes behind it or the amount of problems tackled' (Robinson, 1995: 68).

The reflective Forest School practitioner will be using formal or informal observations to see what the needs of the children are. These are often recorded after the sessions as a part of a reflective session involving all the adults in the group, and are used as a planning tool. The practitioner can then plan subsequent sessions to include opportunities to scaffold and model skills where appropriate. This enables the practitioner to tailor learning and development to the needs of the specific children and the specific event. An important element will be to use dialogue and discussion, listening being more important than talking. This enables the relationships and trust to build between the practitioner and the children.

The next step will be to reflect and transform what we do to incorporate the ethos of Forest School, and through it a new paradigm of supporting development, into all of our early years delivery. In Chapter 7 I will consider further practical ideas for settings to adopt even in our current climate, and in Chapter 8 I will describe some of the exciting ways in which Forest School is being used with other groups.

 Discussion points

In this chapter I have asked you to consider some historical perspectives on early years care and education that may have affected the development of Forest School, and to consider some contemporary ideas that share some characteristics of Forest School. I have reflected on what such an overview can tell us about the place of Forest School in the tides of change that move through early years care and education. You may now be reflecting on some ideas for further synthesis and development. You will find it useful to discuss these with colleagues. The questions below are designed to be prompts to such thinking:

- What philosophies and principles underpin the practice in your setting?
- What are the strengths and weaknesses of each of these?
- Does your recording system match your philosophies and principles?
- Do they equip your children with the skills and strengths to succeed in twenty-first century society?

Further reading

Claxton, G. (2002) *Building Learning Power*. Bristol: TLO.
New Zealand Ministry of Education (1996) *Te Whariki: Early Childhood Curriculum*. Wellington, NZ: Learning Media.
Nicol, J. (2007) *Bringing the Steiner Waldorf Approach to Your Early Years Practice*. London: David Fulton.
Robinson, T. (2001) *Out of Our Minds: Learning to be Creative*. Chichester: Capstone.
Weston, P. (2000) *Friedrich Froebel: His Life, Times and Significance*. 2nd edn. London: Roehampton Institute.

6

Participating in Forest School

Chapter objectives

- To identify the requirements for a Forest School site.
- To consider the requirements for risk assessments for Forest School.
- To describe a typical block of Forest School sessions.
- To consider the skills developed during early Forest School sessions.
- To relate the above objectives to the UK Early Years curricula.

Introduction

In this chapter I intend to draw on my own experiences of running Forest School sessions to illuminate further what Forest School is, and what happens there. Figure 6.1 shows a storytelling area created for me in a local wood.

I will start with a discussion of what to look for when selecting a Forest School site, and then explore risk assessment. This section particularly makes the point that Forest School should be run by qualified Level 3

Figure 6.1   A Forest School storytelling area in the snow, showing how woods are available in all weathers

practitioners and explains why in terms of the training and preparation they follow. I then describe a short block of six Forest School sessions, suitable when the children will then go on to subsequent blocks. Where children only get one chance to participate in Forest School there should be at least 10 sessions. However, by describing six sessions I can show how children's skills in four key areas will develop in that timescale. These key areas are cooperation, self-esteem and confidence, motivation and decision-making, all of which help when the children return to their mainstream settings. I will also link with the UK Early Years curricular so that practitioners can see where Forest School can make a valuable contribution to their delivery of the curriculum.

Selecting a Forest School site

I have run Forest School on four different sites, and have come up with a definition of a perfect site (see Figure 6.2). But perfection is not always possible, and Forest School is very adaptable, as are children. It is worth noting that, as stated previously, the Forestry Commission are committed to providing spaces to run Forest School sessions in all areas of the UK. The Scottish Curriculum for Excellence has set as an outcome for their 3- to 5-year-olds that they enjoy daily opportunities to participate in different kinds of energetic play, both outdoors and indoors (Education Scotland, 2009).

An ideal site:

➢ Plenty of wood to coppice, and to use for activities

➢ Trunks to climb on to extend physical skills and confidence

➢ Rotting wood for discovering minibeasts

➢ Space for exploration and adventure

➢ Light, open environment promoting early confidence

➢ Long trails of ivy, useful for creative activities

➢ Range of trees and plants to investigate

➢ Central glade for easily identified base camp

➢ 10–20 minutes from client groups

➢ Security from roads and access by general public

Figure 6.2   Criteria for an ideal site

I shall now unpick my criteria for an ideal site, and state why I have chosen them.

Plenty of wood to coppice, and to use for activities

It is useful to have plants such as willow, hazel and elder. Elder makes beads, for example, or whistles, as it is relatively easy to remove the pith with a tent peg or skewer. Willow is flexible enough to bend, for weaving or to make crowns. Hazel is easy to peel and make into ornamental wands and so on. Other woods have their uses, and the Level 3 Forest School leadership training encourages participants to find out about these.

Trunks to climb on to extend physical skills and confidence

Tree trunks lying on the ground offer opportunities to practise balancing. Depending on their size, they will take on different roles in imaginative play. If they are of movable size they present opportunities for mathematical engineering, as children find different ways to use them, to make seating around a fire pit or in a den, or to make boats and other props in play.

Rotting wood for discovering minibeasts

We are becoming too tidy outdoors, with the result that some mini-beasts struggle to find homes. Stag beetles, for example, require rotting wood that is left undisturbed for years. It is exciting to build a stag beetle pyramid, by digging a hole and setting logs upright in it to half their depth, then packing the soil back around them. But just allowing a few logs to rot *in situ* gives the children the chance to turn them over (carefully, and then to put them back) to spot the little creatures that will quickly take up residence. Piles of brush-wood will offer cover to a different range of small animals. There is no reason why every site cannot have rotting wood, and all should.

Space for exploration and adventure

The amount of space required depends in part on the age of the chil-dren. The younger the child, the less far they will want to move from wherever you have set up camp, and, indeed, babies will usually stay within the base camp area. In addition, if this is their first opportunity to explore wilder spaces they will not feel confident about going too far from an adult. It will also depend on the number of children in the wood at any one time. The fewer the children, the less space is required. This makes 'space' a subjective concept, and one that will change as children and adults grow in confidence and ability.

Light, open environment promoting early confidence

Again, this is a subjective judgement. Thick, deep forest can be excit-ing to confident 6-year-olds, and scary for 2-year-olds on their first adventure. An open woodland may offer easier access to buggies for very young children. But with enough adult support and proper preparation most woods are exciting enough without being too scary. It is worth remembering that the thicker the wood the colder it will be in summer, and the more sheltered in winter. This and the point about space above constitute a part of the emotional environ-ment (Principles into Practice, 3.3) as well as the physical.

Trails of ivy, useful for creative activities

Do not be put off by a wood that has a flooring of ivy. The base camp area can be cleared for the youngest children, or covered in places by rugs or tarpaulins. The long strands can be woven by children into crowns, camouflage helmets, mobiles and as many other things as their imaginations allow. I put this item in to show that the most unlikely things can be a positive benefit. Level 3 practitioners leading Forest School sessions will be aware of the hazards of poisonous plants and will have planned ways to manage the risks.

Range of trees and plants to investigate

Monoculture can mean bringing in resources to stimulate the children's activities. This can be a problem where Sitka spruce plantations predominate. But even here there may be adjacent areas of scrub where native plants are reclaiming the land. Often elder and hazel are early colonisers, which is fortunate. When looking at potential sites, or planting up new ones, it is a good idea to aim for a range of native plants. Ecologically, environmentally, aesthetically and practically there are advantages to having a range of native plants to access.

Central glade for easily identifiable base camp

'Big' is another subjective term, determined by the age of the children and the group size, but it is an advantage to have an area that is big enough to establish a base camp, and to construct a fire pit without setting fire to overhead branches. Where there are babies and toddlers in the group it is helpful to have space to set down a tarpaulin or rug to crawl from.

10–20 minutes from client groups

This is not always possible, but a goal to work towards. If the site is too far from the client group's base (school, nursery, and so on), then precious time will be lost in transit. The time will, in part, be determined by the mode of transport. A minibus can travel several miles in 20 minutes, but a walking 3-year-old cannot.

Security from roads and access by the general public

Security from roads is an essential safety requirement, clearly. Public access on sites such as those owned by the Forestry Commission and the National Trust may need to be managed with thought and care. I have worked on such a site, although it was a considerable distance from any points of access, so it was only the hardiest of walkers that found us, but it is not ideal. It is better than not having a site to use, but you do need to allow for extra pairs of eyes in your ratios to ensure that the children are safe.

Risk assessment

In other chapters I have emphasised how important it is to children's development that they should be given the opportunity to take reasonable risks. In order to facilitate this, the trained Forest School leader will undertake a wide range of risk assessments. As a part of their Level 3 training they are required to learn about ways to risk assess and what to risk assess. I tend to use the system described below, which gives me a numerical guide to the risk involved in any hazard I have identified. The numbering system is shown here, and the guide for using it in Table 6.1.

Probability (P)	*Consequence (C)*
1 Highly unlikely	1 Slightly harmful
2 Unlikely	2 Harmful
3 Likely	3 Extremely harmful

All statutory settings will have their own methods, which should be followed by the practitioners working within them. The Health and Safety Executive (www.hse.gov.uk) will give guidance on these matters. A Forest School leader will amass a body of evidence to show that all hazards have been considered and accommodated. In this way the Forest School leader sets up an environment that is as safe as it should reasonably be, and which gives children the freedom to

Table 6.1   A risk assessment guide

Probability (P) × Consequence (C) = Risk Rating (RR)

RR	Hazard severity	Action
1	Minimal	No action required, no documentation necessary
2	Acceptable	No extra controls necessary. Alternatives can be considered. Monitoring essential to ensure controls are maintained
3 and 4	Moderate	All avenues should be explored to reduce risk, and implemented within specified time limits
		If a moderate risk is associated with extremely harmful consequences then further assessment is advisable to determine more accurately the probability of harm. This can be used to evaluate the need for improved controls
6	Substantial	Activities should not start until risk has been reduced. If activity already in progress then **urgent** action should be taken
9	Unacceptable	**Activities should not start (or should be stopped) until risk has been reduced.** If this is impossible, the activity must not be carried out

take the risks appropriate to them within that structure. The risk assessment sheets that I have used when none other exists are shown in Figure 6.3. This is an important aspect of the training of a Forest School leader, in order to protect the children but also to protect themselves from prosecution should any accidents occur. Another part of the training is to undertake a first aid course specialising in working outdoors, with the different challenges that this environment can present. All Forest School sessions that take place on sites that are not the usual school or nursery settings should therefore be led by Forest School leaders trained to Level 3.

A typical block of Forest School sessions

If children are only going to have one block of Forest School sessions, settings should aim to book at least 10 weekly sessions of half a day in duration. The benefits of Forest School have been shown to increase over time. The Early Years Interboard Panel in Northern Ireland have published a handbook for practitioners describing how to provide outdoor experiences for young children every day (Bratton et al., 2005). Forest School is about facilitating long-term change and, to do that, settings need to commit to a minimum of 10 weeks.

Many settings now are looking at arranging a year-long programme of Forest School. Where this is possible, and the setting breaks their year into terms, six weeks per term fits conveniently into the year and allows time for the other annual events in the school or nursery curriculum. I have described below some outcomes and reflections on a six-week programme for an early years class of 3- and 4-year-old children for their first term of Forest School.

Preliminaries
Before starting I present an 'Introduction to Forest Schools' to the parents/carers and staff of the children I will be working with, as an evening event in the previous term, allowing time for discussion of concerns. Parents are also given an open invitation to join any of the sessions. The Welsh Foundation Phase Curriculum 'promotes equality of opportunity and values, and celebrates diversity. Positive partnerships with the home are fostered and an appreciation of parents/carers as the children's first educators is acknowledged' (Welsh Assembly, 2008). We recruit sufficient teaching assistants and volunteers to keep our ratios at no more than 1:6 early years professionals to children, preferably lower.

Figure 6.3 Risk assessment sheets

Seasonal Site Risk Assessments

Site:

Assessed by:

Date assessed:

Signature:

	Define hazard	P	C	RR	Hazard severity	Action	Review date
Mobile phone signal:							
Boundaries:							
Tree layer (tree types):							
Shrub layer (types of lower branches of mature trees and small trees/large shrubs):							
Field layer (clearing, ground cover, ferns, animal habitats):							
Ground layer (mosses, fungi, leaf mould):							
Others (e.g. ponds/streams, ditches, seating, overhead power cables):							

Photocopiable:
Forest School and Outdoor Learning in the Early Years, 2nd Edition, SAGE Publications © Sara Knight, 2013

Figure 6.3 (*Continued*)

Activity Risk Assessment

Site: Date assessed:

Accessed by: Signature:

Activity list for the day	Define hazard	P	C	RR	Hazard severity	Action	Review date
Accessing site							

Photocopiable:
Forest School and Outdoor Learning in the Early Years, 2nd Edition, SAGE Publications © Sara Knight, 2013

(*Continued*)

Figure 6.3 *(Continued)*

Daily Site Check

Site: Date assessed:

Assessed by: Signature:

Four-level risk check	Define hazard	P	C	RR	Hazard severity	Action	Review date
High-level risks: Canopy							
Branches							
Other							
Medium-level risks: Bushes							
Branches							
Other							
Ground cover risks: Plants							
Obstacles							
Soil Level:							

Photocopiable:
Forest School and Outdoor Learning in the Early Years, 2nd Edition, SAGE Publications © Sara Knight, 2013

Figure 6.3 (Continued)

Assessment of children with EBD

Child's name:

Session/group:

DOB:

Location:

Likely triggers	Predicted response	P	C	RR	Intervention and de-escalation Strategies	Review date

Photocopiable:
Forest School and Outdoor Learning in the Early Years, 2nd Edition, SAGE Publications © Sara Knight, 2013

I carry out a seasonal site risk assessment a few weeks before starting the programme. This allows time for repairs and maintenance work to be carried out. A copy of this form is given to the setting. As I plan each session I complete a risk assessment for the activities we will be offering the children. Copies of these forms and my planning sheets are given to the staff I will be working with in advance, to allow them time to plan follow-up activities. Before each session I go to the wood and carry out a daily site risk assessment, which I carry with me. This is a requirement for all UK practitioners, as can be seen in the Scottish *Curriculum for Excellence* (Education Scotland, 2009).

We will have about two hours in the wood for each session. I try in my planning to create a repetitive framework starting with setting up the shelters each week. This is turning a necessity to an advantage. This site is susceptible to trespass, and leaving the shelters up would be an invitation to interference. Asking the children to help set up the shelters establishes and reinforces the ideas that they are able to carry out these active tasks, have ownership of the site, have a degree of autonomy over what happens, and that we are here and ready to go. This routine is a wake-up which alerts the children that they will be learning using all their senses and all of their bodies. Similarly, the patterns at the end of the session signal a return to conventional school rules and ways of behaving. Within the session there are opportunities for cooperation, safety awareness, decision-making, ownership of tasks, and so on. These aim to promote self-esteem, confidence and self-motivation, which are the skills I hope they will transfer back into school life.

The central core of each session is as child initiated and child led as the children wish. I plan a range of activities to offer around a theme of developing sensory awareness. As this is their first block of sessions, it provides a good basis for their developing self and environmental awareness. The activities are optional. The children are at different stages of confidence and ability, and some already have their own agenda about how to respond to the natural world. The ratios enable sensitive observations and, where invited, interventions to extend and develop ideas. The less confident children value the chance to participate in the activities we provide, although I know that over time they, too, will develop their own priorities in the wood. Table 6.2 is an overview of the six sessions, with the learning objectives stated briefly.

Session one

Unpacking my rucksack: the children take it in turns to remove and describe an item. This gives the children time to explore the likely events in Forest School, and the expectations we have of them, and they of us. The first aid box and wipes prompt a discussion on safety – they state basic safety rules that apply in school, such as not touching things, staying in a line and holding hands. I encourage them to think about when we might want to stick to those rules and when we might want to change them, for example when we are working in the wood, and say that I would teach them some new safety games to help in that situation. Waterproofs and tarpaulins lead into a discussion about the weather, and they are keen to tell me about the clothing they have

Table 6.2 A block of six Forest School sessions

Week	Activity	Learning objectives
1	**School based:**	Familiarisation with staff
	Introduction to staff	Familiarisation with verbal and visual prompts
	Introduction to safety games	
	Walk around wood	To encourage fun outside
		To show an awareness of space, of themselves and of others
		Recognise the changes that happen to their bodies when they are active
		To promote curiosity, interest and communication with others
	Make map sticks	Use a range of materials to create representational images
	Story and song	Listen to a story, compose a song
2	**School based:**	Rehearse verbal and visual prompts
	Rehearse safety games	Continue to be interested, excited and motivated to learn
	Discuss health and safety (fungi and berries, etc.)	
		Familiarise with learning environment
	Wood based (houses, homes and bases):	Use their creative imaginations
		Problem-solving and decision-making
	Set boundaries	Taking turns, share and exercise self-control
	Establish base and shelter	
	Circle time and snack	Be confident to try new activities
	Talk about and look for other animals' homes	Begin to appreciate the importance of their environment
	Making bugs and spiders	Share group song as created last week
	Song to close (story if time)	

(Continued)

Table 6.2 Continued

Week	Activity	Learning objectives
3, 4, 5 **Select:** **For any day**	Reinforce prior learning **Visual exploration:** Finding sticks Drawing with sticks or Searching for landmarks Natural colours Visual exploration – big/small, large/tall Circle time and snack Dreamcatchers	Investigate natural environment Continue to be interested, excited and motivated to learn Promoting close observation and concentration Move confidently increasing control and coordination Communicate needs Make choices and initiate ideas Explore colour, light, size and shape
For a wet day	**Auditory exploration:** Natural music search Creating an instrument Walking quietly game Tracking signs Circle time and snack Prepare for poetry-making Song to close	Investigate natural environment Continue to be interested, excited and motivated to learn Recognise and explore how sounds can be changed Close observation and concentration Communicate needs Exercise self-control Exploring descriptive words
For a warmer day	**Smell and feel exploration:** Smell search Making webs Weaving Tree hugging and rubbing Circle time and snack Use of potato peelers Song to close	Investigate natural environment Continue to be interested, excited and motivated to learn Promoting close observation and concentration Communicate needs Exercise self-control Use small tools with increasing control Observe safe use of tools (secateurs or loppers) Explore and experiment
6	**Closure session:** Prepare a fire and light it Make a woven calendar of six weeks Explore to find own special place – explore and describe its smell, look and feel Circle time and toast marshmallows Clear base and shelter area Back to classroom for story and songs	Respond to significant experiences, showing a range of feelings when appropriate Develop awareness of own needs, views and feelings, and those of others Developing respect for own cultures and beliefs and those of other people Form good relationships with adults and peers Recognise the importance of keeping healthy and what has contributed to this at FS Share group song and memories

been sent with for the day. The bag of assorted thicknesses of cord and the small tools are of great interest, and they are very serious about the idea that if I can trust them to be sensible then they will get to use them.

Safety games on the playing field: these include '1, 2, 3, where are you?', a call that can be used by adult and children alike to locate everyone, who respond by jumping up and down and waving their arms, calling '1, 2, 3, over here!' This game is used in every Forest School I have ever visited. Quickly they accept that failure to conform to these safety requirements will result in everyone returning to the class – I do not have to carry out the threat, they take me seriously. As the Welsh Curriculum points out, 'Children are supported in becoming confident, competent and independent thinkers and learners . . . They experience challenges that extend their learning' (Welsh Assembly, 2008).

A walk around the wood (it is not large), and then into the centre of the wood where there is a suitable clearing. There is a frisson of excitement that here is something new, and they are all attentive. I tell them that next week we will return here and make a base camp before we do other activities. They are not sure what a base camp is, but it sounds good. I say that we will have to find our way back, and that means remembering landmarks. I explain this in terms of the North American native people's map sticks (in our case, rectangles of card with slots cut in them), and say that they can make one of these on the way back to the classroom. I show them how to slot things into the cuts in the card, and we discuss safety issues (thorns and nettles) and environmental issues (flowers). We help the children to make their map sticks as we slowly wind our way back to the classroom.

We have begun to construct a framework within which Forest School will occur – the routines that signal to the child that this is Forest School time. I have begun to give them signals about what Forest School will (and will not) be. Taking time to set up a framework in this way helps children to feel secure, and when they are secure they feel more like taking risks and exploring their own capabilities, overriding the animal instinct to hold something in reserve in case you need to 'fight or flight' in an unknown environment. The importance of boundaries is explained in Early Years Foundation Stage, Principles into Practice, 1.3.

Session two

When I arrive in class the children sing me the song they have worked out with their teacher:

To the Woods

(tune – 'If you're happy and you know it')

Oh we're off to play our games in the wood (clap clap)

Oh we're off to play our games in the wood (clap clap)

Oh we're off to play our games

Playing safely as we should

Oh we're off to play our games in the wood (clap clap)

It is a good choice as it is one that we can easily make up extra verses to.

We do not stick to the plan above. Flexibility is essential in Forest School, and you will need to constantly observe and reflect on the children's needs. When we get to the centre of the wood the children stand around awaiting instructions – not ready to initiate action yet! They find the heap of long poles on my prompting, and we discuss safe ways to carry long poles – although they are not heavy, it is better to have two children, one at each end, to stop the ends waving around. During the construction of the tipi the children take more and more control, as they learn the skills and gain the confidence. Two boys start a game with sticks, and we have a chat about when it is and is not safe to wave them about at head height. Sticks are an important part of being outside, and it is better to use them safely than not use them at all. We discuss marking a 'safe' area by tying orange tapes to the trees. The children have the tapes, and run to where they think it will be safe, and then the adults tie them. As there is a lot of ground ivy to trip over, there are a lot of tumbles, but no one seems to mind.

We chat about who else might live in the wood. We hear a pheasant, but otherwise the children are unsure. I suggest that they go to look for signs such as holes, but their wanderings are vague until one child spots a 'hole' in a heap of brambles and brushwood. He is excited, and convinced that there is a hedgehog asleep in there. This galvanises the others, and we find a more plausible hole (although probably not the badger they hoped for – I suggest a rabbit), several old birds' nests, and some minibeasts under a log. One boy wants to look in an 'unsafe' part of the wood (that is, outside the boundary tape), and so I go with him and a couple of other boys. He finds a run into some thick cover that has been made by a larger animal, and we discuss this. The idea of other creatures living in their wood excites them enormously, and it is an idea they returned to in subsequent weeks.

After snack, they have some time for the undirected play that is not happening unprompted as yet. Some nice 'home' games started in the lean-to, and the teaching assistant was asked to help in the construction of an imaginary cooking pot over a fire. As Garrick (2004: 32) says, children 'need time to explore . . . supported by adults who are sensitive to the value of independence and self-directed activity'.

Session three

When I get to the wood for my morning risk assessment I find that workmen have been into the wood and felled two large trees, cut the trunks and large branches into logs, and chipped the rest, leaving two large piles of chippings. The class teacher and I find whatever we can by way of spades, wheelbarrows and buckets and make them available should the children choose to use them. We also have a head teacher from another local primary school observing, so we get her engaged, too.

Getting the shelters up is getting quicker. The children are confident about getting themselves into pairs, and queue to present their poles to me. Sorting out which way up they go leads to some interesting interactions! 'Experiences . . . become embedded into episodic memories in the brain, to be reactivated and used in later learning' (Bruce, 2004: 126).

The children decide to use the chips to refresh the path around the outside of the wood, but not their own path to the base camp, which they want to keep secret and special. As the Northern Ireland booklet states, 'Children need to be able to control, change and modify their environment' (Bratton et al., 2005: 11). They work hard on the task, joining and leaving it as they want to. This is key to enabling the children to realise the freedom that they have to determine their own actions, and to contribute to group decisions. Two boys compare the length of a log to a space by lying beside the log and space to measure it with their body lengths, and three other boys work out how to manoeuvre a heavy log by collaborative pushing. 'Rich learning cannot be rushed. Developing learning means that through the senses and movement children build their understanding of time, space and the reason for things' (Bruce, 2004: 127). Another negotiation initiated by the children is that one of the chipping heaps is outside the 'safe' area, so they ask us to move the ribbons to make the area bigger. We agree.

We run over time, so we only have time for one verse of our song on our return. At the end, the visiting head teacher pronounces that she is looking at 'a class of satisfied children'. We touched the spirit of Forest School today, with the children in charge and the adults there to support and facilitate their success. Fisher (1996: 74) identified the benefits of involving children in decision-making, as we did today, and it sums up the benefits of Forest School:

- Gives opportunities for real-life problem-solving.

- Encourages them to maintain something which they have planned.

- Enables them to have an element of control over their own learning environment.

- Leads to the development of organisation as a life skill.

- Gives them a sense of responsibility/self-esteem.

- Encourages cooperation and collaboration between them and adults.

- Enables the teacher to see things from the children's perspective.

Session four

A rainy day: the children are keen to get the shelters up, and are now equal partners in the process. I offer materials for dreamcatchers, and also suggest that if they did not want to do these, they might think about the sounds in the wood. I work with four boys who are keen to move out of the safe area towards the top (wilder) area in search of logs to line the path. This includes the most energetic children, who burn an amazing amount of energy with their persistence and effort.

At snack time I drum on a fallen log. One of the children says that he can make a noise scrunching on the leaves, and proceeds to demonstrate jumping in a heap of fallen leaves. We congratulate his find. Another boy says that he can make a noise running through a patch of sycamore whips, whipping them with a stick. This is an interesting noise, and we debate how to describe it. This sparks more interest, and children spend time experimenting with sounds and ways to describe them. The teacher is planning to use their ideas as prompts to poetry-making during the rest of the week.

I offer to show anyone who is interested where they could make pictures. One or two were, so we clear a patch and start creating. Others join us, and the artwork becomes more impressive as they experiment. In another area, one child starts drilling with his stick, and this progresses to a complex game of excavation engaging several children. The holes become canals, then rivers, then I'm not sure what, with bridges and stone linings in places. The lack of water does not seem to bother the children.

We also offer potato peelers to remove the bark from sticks. Some Forest School leaders believe that tools should only be used for the purpose for which they were designed, in this case peeling vegetables. In general I agree, but in England it is rare for children to have experienced sharp tool use at a young age, and using peelers in this way enables them to experience the basic rules of tool use in comparative safety.

We discuss which is the best wood for peeling, and what the wood smells like when peeled, and some children go off to 'look for smells' – this turns into some deep play. Different children find the peeling easier or harder, but all are engaged with the task, and determined to achieve. The benefit of Forest School is that every child can tackle the activities at their own level. One child who finds it hard to concentrate in class works on his stick for an hour. Bilton (2003: 12) quotes evidence that 'when children are given time to work at an activity, they can concentrate for a considerable period of time'. Three of the other boys move around the camp, sitting in different places, but continuing with the task for most of the session.

Session five

Role play, the way in which children make sense of their world: one child is engaged with the tipi as a miniature house, and is absorbed with those details of coverings and linings. Another is concerned with the structural elements of propping up a number of sticks at the appropriate angle. Two others have found ivy-covered trunks in a V formation that become a boat. This boat has some fantastic voyages, and other children join and leave the game as it unrolls. The only adult intervention needed is when pirates invade and want to re-route the boat against the wishes of the original owners. I am able to mediate a compromise that gives the pirates a temporary lift (saving face) before they move off elsewhere. In Forest Schools the adults are acting as facilitators and providers, and intervene as sensitively as possible into the process. In this example one of the learning oppor-tunities is the social learning that is taking place, cooperating and negotiating with one another, and unnecessary adult intervention would diminish the value of the play. I only step in when one child becomes distressed by the activities of a group that sought to domi-nate the play that she had started.

Session six

There has been a storm in between the sessions, so there were fallen branches across the path they had worked on: the children are very excited about having 'a real fire', but the storm damage puts it out of their heads. Some of them are surprised, some shocked. I feel it is a powerful lesson, not only about the power of the weather, but also that there is not always someone to blame for events, there are just things that happen. We spend time deciding how to clear the fallen branches safely, and how to work in a team to achieve this. Then we have to decide where to put them.

Eventually we are sorted and camped, and start collecting wood for our fire. They are good at sorting out dead from live wood, and we soon have piles of different sizes. Marshmallow-toasting is a great suc-cess. It seems a natural way to round off our sessions together. On our return I have hugs and a special card. I read them *Where the Forest Meets the Sea*, another special adventure to think about. It is a fitting end to our block of Forest School sessions, and links to the Early Years Foundation Stage, Principles into Practice, 2.1, Respecting Each Other.

Only later do I find out how worried the staff were about having a fire – no one is as confident as they appear! But they trusted me, and by participating in the activity they achieved too.

The skills developed during early Forest School sessions

Four areas of skill development are apparent after running even these first sessions. They are cooperation, self-esteem and confidence, motivation and decision-making. These are all key skills for conventional learning, and teachers report that they can see classroom improvement in all of the children. In the group described above this can be summarised in the following way:

1 **Cooperation**. The children can all negotiate with each other and with adults to achieve desired goals – they had these skills before, but they are now enhanced. One dominant child is beginning to accommodate the needs of others into his active and direct way of operating. This links to the Early Years Foundation Stage, Principles into Practice, 2.1, Respecting Each Other.

2 **Self-esteem and confidence**. Children who were not stars before now know that they can twinkle in their own ways – they have all found new talents and abilities.

3 **Motivation**. Two boys in particular have found a depth of interest in the environment and been able to explore that interest. They can draw on that interest and knowledge in their future learning.

4 **Decision-making**. All of the children have grown in their ability to take decisions in their play and in negotiation with one another in Forest School tasks. Their abilities for 'self esteem, independence, confidence, dispositions to learning, sound skills and team work' (Bratton et al., 2005: 26) have greatly improved.

 Discussion points

In this chapter I started with a discussion of what to look for when selecting a Forest School site, and went on to explore what, how and why to risk assess. Drawing on my own experience I then described six Forest School sessions. This enabled me to show how children's skills in four key areas can develop in that timescale. These are cooperation, self-esteem and confidence, motivation and decision-making, all of which help when the children return to their mainstream settings. I also made reference throughout to the different Early Years curricula in the UK, although not exhaustively. You may wish to discuss these points further. Here is a brief summary of the three points:

(Continued)

(Continued)

1 There are 10 points to consider when selecting a Forest School site. While they are not all essential, they are all worthy of consideration. Your setting may have some of these already, even if it is not a wood.

2 Carrying out exhaustive risk assessments is essential in order to create a space in which children can take the risks that are appropriate to their age and stage of development. Training is needed to know not only how to assess, but also what to assess and when. The Level 3 in Forest School leadership is specialist training that enables an individual to do this, one of the reasons why they should lead Forest School sessions.

3 During early Forest School sessions the children move from needing direction to being self-motivating with their own agenda and priorities. The adults can then move to being facilitators and observers. This encourages the development of cooperation, self-esteem and confidence, motivation and decision-making. You may be able to do this in your settings.

Further reading

Callaway, C. (2005) *The Early Years Curriculum: A View from Outdoors*. London: David Fulton.

Casey, T. (2007) *Environments for Outdoor Play*. London: Paul Chapman.

Davis, B., Rea, T. and Waite, S. (2006) 'The special nature of the outdoors: its contribution to the education of children aged 3–11', *Australian Journal of Outdoor Education*, 10(2): 3–12.

Waite, S. (ed.) (2011) *Children Learning Outside the Classroom*. London: Sage.

7

Getting the Forest School Ethos into Settings

Chapter objectives

- To consider what can be distilled from Forest School and applied to all settings.
- To suggest ways in which the ethos of Forest School can be incorporated into the outdoor play of all settings.
- To set out some simple steps towards achieving Forest School-type activities in settings.

Introduction

It would be wonderful if every child could have access to Forest School, but for the foreseeable future it is not likely that this will happen. Even for 3- and 4-year-olds provision is patchy, although it is spreading, and for younger and older children it is even more thinly spread. It is therefore up to individual settings to take what they can from the best of Forest School and incorporate it into their outdoor regimes. In this way all children can benefit from a consideration of what is the specialness of Forest School and how some of that can be introduced into all outdoor play provision. In the next chapter we will consider some projects that are helping older children, and in this chapter we will consider how all early years practitioners can develop their practice in the Foundation Stage/Phase towards supporting Forest School activities in their own settings.

How some aspects of Forest School relate to all outdoor play

To distil the specialness of Forest School it is necessary to return to a consideration of what makes a Forest School different from other outdoor experiences. Having done that, we can consider three issues: what are the Forest School headings that are a part of normal onsite outdoor play? What are areas for development under the different Early Years Curricula in the UK? What things do settings need to address to add Forest School activities to their offering?

In Chapter 2, I described the ethos of Forest School under the following headings:

1 The setting is not the usual one.

2 The Forest School is made as safe as is reasonably possible, in order to facilitate children's risk-taking.

3 Forest School happens over time.

4 There is no such thing as bad weather, only bad clothing.

5 Trust is central.

6 The learning is play based and, as far as possible, child initiated and child led.

7 The blocks and the sessions have beginnings and ends.

8 The sessions are run by a trained Forest School leader.

Item 5 would hopefully be irrelevant where children are playing in their usual setting with their usual carers. Items 3, 4 and 7 were addressed by the 2008 Early Years Foundation Stage Curriculum, which stated that all children up to the end of their fifth year should go outside at some point every day, which led to many settings enabling free-flow play between indoors and outdoors. The consequence of this should be that many settings for this age group are able to provide sufficient outdoor access so that children can freely engage with the outdoor environment in tune with their own interests and rhythms, and those settings enable children to experience rain, shine, and all the other variations of weather that make up their environment. Similarly, the other countries in the UK have early years curricula that emphasise the importance of outdoor provision in the early years.

For these changes to take place, willing settings may need to make changes to their premises, but often change can start through smaller alterations, to things such as attitude and planning. Adult attitudes to the outdoors as a part of the normal learning environment can help to make big changes. Regarding outdoors as a learning environment with equal validity to indoors requires a culture shift starting with a revision of attitudes to the weather. As soon as adults in settings are prepared to be outside in all weathers, the children will be willing to follow suit. It is the adults who do not wish to be outside in extreme weather conditions, not the children. But the adult role is to make access in all weathers a practical possibility. I have already described how babies in Denmark and other countries are outside in their prams in all weathers, and 50 years ago that was the norm in this country, too. We may need to consider how to insulate modern prams to previous standards to ensure that babies are warm enough, and we may need to provide more robust outdoor clothing for crawlers and toddlers. When there is a demand, manufacturers will follow, as can be seen by the greater number of all-weather suits available for older children. Until then, ideas for sourcing items will be discussed later in this chapter.

Making changes to planning regimes means incorporating the outdoor space into the same set of plans as the indoor space. Whatever planning schemes are used, the way in which the different spaces are utilised expresses the attitudes and values of the setting. For example, if mark-making equipment is available indoors and outdoors in a setting, then the outdoor space is probably seen as a learning environment, not just a space for letting off steam. Children will pick up on these attitudes. As Louv (2005: 14) has said, children are sensitive to the unspoken and hidden messages from adult behaviour. It is therefore important to communicate through the hidden curriculum that the outdoor space, and thus by inference the environment, is a valued space that should be engaged with. Planning, a process that children are not always included in, is usually a part of that hidden agenda.

For older children in school settings the introduction of Forest School requires a creative use of the curriculum, but this is happening in many places. And the government requirement for schools to provide wrap-around care (DCSF, 2005) enables playworkers to consider offering opportunities for children to engage in Forest School activities in after-school and holiday clubs. The ethos of Forest School is congruent with the values of Playwork, and the practical ideas described below should be of interest to those working with older children.

Incorporating the other aspects of Forest School into outdoor play

Taking out the elements of the Forest School ethos discussed above leaves four elements still to consider, one by one. Under each heading I will discuss things that might be done immediately, and things that can be planned for:

1 The setting is not the usual one.

2 The Forest School is made as safe as is reasonably possible, in order to facilitate children's risk-taking.

3 The learning is play based and, as far as possible, child initiated and child led.

4 The sessions are run by a trained Forest School leader.

The setting is not the usual one

Taking children out of their usual setting creates an atmosphere of magic or secrecy or separateness, or all three. Trees have an additional magic of their own, and can create spaces which stimulate the imagination. This atmosphere enables creativity and frees the child to explore physically and mentally. Voyages can be travelled, stories spun, and the senses can be stimulated in many ways. In order to emulate this atmosphere, practitioners may need to think laterally.

It is worth considering whether you have a shed with a space behind it, as this instantly creates a separate space. It does not have to be a large space, or tidied up, provided that the adults in the setting are comfortable that there are no unmanageable hazards there. There does need to be an element of trust, however, that the children can play unseen at times and that adults will not intrude uninvited. Often a shed will be sited quite close to a boundary, enabling a tarpaulin to be placed over the gap, providing shade or shelter in extreme weather conditions. Once the space has become established as a play area, practitioners can check how it is stimulating deep play by suspending a tape recorder from the shed roof from time to time (but be aware of the ethics of how you use such data). Many children's stories start with secret places in gardens, from the Flowerpot Men to the Secret Garden.

Alternatively, areas can be screened off in a variety of simple ways. Garden centres often have rolls of split cane or rush that can be stretched between a fence and a single upright post. Or you can make a screen by growing runner beans in pots and up canes stuck into them. Natural materials such as these have a sensory quality of their own that adds to the space you are creating. Again, the areas do not need to be large. If you are providing for younger children, the space needs to be just big enough for a small rug or mat for them to lie on. In any case, it is advisable to provide some shade from May to October, as young children's skins are more sensitive to sun damage than adult skin, and a part of the shade screening can be incorporated into the creation of that special space where children can access their environment nose to nose.

Children's favourite special places are often the dens they have created for themselves, so you can provide den-making equipment and leave it to the experts, the children themselves. They will ask for your help if they need it. Dens can be made out of old cardboard boxes, or planks and large construction equipment, or tarpaulins, or old sheets and string. Consider whether they need to be cleared away at the end of the day, or can be left to evolve creatively as the children and the weather interact together.

Magic carpets can be their own space. This may require an initiating adult, to introduce the idea that once on the carpet children can go wherever they wish, do whatever they wish, and then return again. In my nursery we had a small rug for this purpose, and once the illusion had been created the children would walk around in their own imaginary world completely divorced from the other games around them, until they had 'flown home'. This was fine until we had a child with Asperger's syndrome in the setting, who was terrified of the carpet! Having difficulty with imaginary ideas, and a tendency to take things literally, he was afraid that the carpet really would transport him to strange places, and he would be lost and unable to get home. However, he desperately wanted to join in his friends' games. We coped with a slow process of desensitisation, whereby one of us would sit with him and watch the magic carpet play, narrating the events and answering his questions. The next stage was to explore the carpet on a one-to-one basis, and then to slowly engage him in the play, until eventually he could participate.

With some creative thinking it is often possible to help children to find a space that is magic or secret or separate. Once it is created, practitioners need to respect the specialness of the space, and help those not engaged with it to do the same. This is harder to do when you are in your usual setting, as it requires greater sensitivity on the part of the non-engaged person, big or small, to remember what is happening. The space will not work as a separate and magical place, however, unless this can occur. This means that the other sorts of equipment that might intrude where space is limited, such as wheeled toys and balls, may need to have a different designated spot – perhaps indoors?

The long-term goal might be to provide permanent dividers in the space. These could be wooden fences or log rolls, or changes of level. This leads into the next area, to consider safety issues. Planting a tree to create a space is another option, although it is advisable to take advice to determine the best tree for the size of your plot and its proximity to buildings. Subsidence can be caused by root damage from too big a tree.

The Forest School is made as safe as is reasonably possible, in order to facilitate children's risk-taking

Mortlock (2000: 22) describes the ideal state for learning outdoors as one of adventure: 'the person feels in control of the situation, but is using his experience and abilities to overcome a technical problem'. That state may be achieved very differently by children of different ages, by going into a strange wood, or by balancing on a log. Re-creating that state in children's usual setting so that all children of all ages can test their boundaries offers practitioners an interesting set of challenges. This is particularly true if at the same time you are trying to make the experience relevant to the natural environment, in order to create Forest School-type activities.

For very young children, contact with the environment will be a holistic and sensory one. If they still retain the need to mouth objects in order to understand them, then there will be risk enough in outdoor heuristic play. Fir cones, stones, shells and other non-poisonous natural objects too large to swallow will fascinate and engross young children as they learn that some things taste better than others and perhaps a visual inspection sometimes does the trick. Different surfaces will also expand their world, although it is nice to have a rug to crawl back to. Sand, grass and earth are natural elements that all children need access to if they are to learn about their world, and how to move around in it safely. Practitioners have noted that more young children are now unstable walkers on surfaces other than concrete and carpet. Offering these different surfaces from an early age will help these abilities to develop.

As children become more mobile they will appreciate their natural objects in more portable forms. Young children love to sort stones and pebbles into innumerable groupings of size, shape, colour, and categories withheld from adults but known by them. Providing baskets to put them in can add an aesthetic as well as practical quality, and the risk element is in the increased range of resources, diminishing in actual size. Another favourite activity is transporting objects around, and so practitioners can add the risk factors of wheeled transportation. In Chapter 6, I described how we moved bark chippings around the forest. The children with the greatest prior experience of using wheelbarrows and trolleys were those least likely to run over fingers or crash into other workers on the paths. Facilitating the moving around of sand, mud, stones, bark and other natural features can challenge practitioners who prefer to keep these materials within separate boundaries, but the risk to order and tidiness is less important than the learning opportunities offered by a certain degree of chaos, otherwise known as scientific discovery.

Water is a welcome risk which can be added to sand, earth, and so on. Water play offers endless opportunities for creativity. In addition to static holders of water, sections of guttering to the outdoor equipment give children a chance to move water around the space, creating flow and falls, puddles and bog. Portable water, for example in watering cans and kettles, offers imaginative opportunities, perhaps to add to potions. The real risks to children are minimal, although it is likely that there will be wet and muddy clothing.

Creating different levels in a setting can increase the amount of space available. Where there is a mound there can be a space beneath it. Where there is a slope there is a saving of the space needed for a slide – it can be built into the earth. Different levels can create different risks. For young children it can be about managing their own mobility up and down in different ways. For older children it can be about managing the mobility of objects, rolling or riding them. For wheelchair users and those with restricted mobility, changes of levels on site offer opportunities to experiment with the challenges that they will face in the wider community. It can also provide opportunities for dropping objects off edges, thus learning about gravity and velocity. Again, the space does not have to be huge, but the benefits to physical and spatial development can be.

If earth moving is a long-term goal, a short-term solution can be a felled tree or large log. In truth, this is a good addition to any setting, providing opportunities for climbing, balancing and hiding behind. This is no longer a regular experience for all children, particularly in urban settings, so providing it within the setting is very beneficial. It is of lasting benefit, too, in that as it degrades it will provide homes for a fascinating range of minibeasts for the children to watch and

Figure 7.1   An example of an impromptu pulley

investigate. Large rocks can be used in similar ways – while they do not degrade, minibeasts will still shelter in their cool shade. Existing trees offer opportunities for impromptu and temporary height changes using home-made pulleys, as can be seen in Figure 7.1.

True Forest School opportunities involve lighting fires. There are safety precautions, but Forest School practitioners will enable all participants to sit safely beside a fire, and usually help to cook or make a drink. This is a normal thing to do in cultures closer to nature than the majority of the British population. Many modern children do not have this experience – one 4-year-old asked a colleague who had lit a fire if that meant that it was Guy Fawkes Night. This was his only experience of fire. Trained Forest School leaders will be comfortable with having a fire pit in their setting, but others may not. Yet fire is elemental, and fascinating. Without the experience of safe fire, children may put themselves in danger. Practitioners should consider whether they can cook outside over a fire in a contained way if they do not have the confidence or the space for a fire pit. Making and eating soup from local vegetables cooked over their own fire is a wonderful experience for children.

I hope that this section has shown that risks are comparative, and should be age appropriate, and that the risks appropriate to many preschool children are well within the scope of most settings to provide. I have focused on those risks associated with Forest School activities and the environment, but other risky opportunities can be provided in other ways. Thinking about risk in a new way may involve educating parents, practitioners and other staff about the necessity for risk-taking. This may include training staff in risk assessment, and ultimately in writing a new risk assessment policy, thinking more about allowing for reasonable risks.

In the long term, settings may consider landscaping to provide different levels, downs as well as ups. Fire pits are features of many Scandinavian settings, but can be replaced by the purchase of a container for a fire – there are a number of designs possible. Water features that enable children to move water around the space are exciting ideas for which to plan.

The learning is play based and, as far as possible, child initiated and child led

The Early Years Foundation Stage Curriculum (DfES, 2007) states that practitioners should 'observe children to find out about their needs, what they are interested in and what they can do'. This is a fundamental part of Forest School, and one that enables practitioners to provide children with the resources they need to initiate and lead play. It is one of the shared perspectives of Reggio Emilia, Steiner and Forest School curricula, and also of all of the UK Early Years curricula.

Being child initiated and child led gives practitioners plenty of opportunities to observe and reflect, and gives the children plenty of opportunities to create, share and develop ideas. It requires practitioners to be sensitive and empathetic to the children's play needs. Providing new resources may also mean providing the knowledge and skills of how to use them, so there will be periods of adult-led activities, but children can indicate from their levels of involvement when they are ready to take those resources and make them their own. They may invite participation by adults, or ask for assistance in specific tasks, but practitioners need to remember when it is the children's game, and when they are therefore only there by invitation.

Watching such play is a privilege. Absorbing deep play helps children to understand about the qualities and properties of the world around them. This play may be solitary, but be no less important for that. It may also be creative, as they represent the world they are investigating. For example, I have watched a boy re-create a tree with a bird's nest in it on the ground using twigs (see Figures 7.2 and 7.3). Once he had completed his self-appointed task he lost interest in what was to me a work of art. It had fulfilled its function in helping him to understand what he had seen, and was therefore redundant. Such play needs time, time to think through the processes of their own learning, and accommodate new abstract concepts.

Child-led play usually has a strong social element. It is in such play that children engage in social negotiation, learning the rules of how society works and how to perform within it. Interestingly, in Forest School it has been observed that girls and boys play together more often, which is when they are using natural materials in natural settings. Practitioners may also observe similar play if they provide natural materials in a natural area of their setting. An example of this can be seen in Figures 7.4 and 7.5, where providing a bucket of mud resulted in decorating a tree with muddy faces.

Figure 7.2 The nests in trees that inspired the creativity described

Figure 7.3 The resultant artwork

Figure 7.4   Using mud to create muddy faces (natural model-making)

A long-term goal for settings could be to create more natural spaces in their settings, and to incorporate opportunities for more child-initiated and child-led play to occur. Shared storytelling is also a feature of such play, with narratives that may continue despite breaks over prolonged periods. These extended narratives appear to be a part of establishing the children's ownership of sites, and are a fascinating study in their own right, as recorded by Tim Waller (2006; 2007).

The sessions are run by a trained Forest School leader

Running Forest School requires you to be a Level 3 Forest School practitioner, although you can experiment with Forest School activities where appropriate. And the Level 1 Forest Skills award can be taken in two days, and will give practitioners a wealth of ideas to draw upon, as well as linking them in to the web of Forest School provision. As can be seen from Figure 7.6, participants are given the opportunity to learn about a range of activities! All practitioners delivering Early Years curricula will benefit from input on how to enhance their environmental awareness, and their awareness of the impact that being in their natural environment can have on children.

Seeking funding and opportunities for training could be a long-term goal for practitioners. Including such training in plans for continuing professional development will help this to become a reality.

Figure 7.5 The resultant muddy faces stuck to a tree

Figure 7.6 A range of tools for use on a Level 1 training course

Achieving Forest School-type activities in settings

In this section I will consider some practical suggestions for making Forest School activities possible in settings. Many of these have been collected from practitioners who are participating in Forest School activities, or who plan to do so in the near future. They are applicable to provision for all preschool children, irrespective of age.

Equipment – things that can be done immediately

Ask parents and friends to donate pairs of wellington boots that have been grown out of. Peg pairs together and store upside down to prevent 'visitors' such as spiders, from taking up residence. Collect spares of appropriate clothing and footwear; socks are particularly useful, as wellington boots are cold in winter. Similarly, winter hats – as many believe that the greatest heat loss is out of the top of the head – and summer hats if the area used is not sufficiently shady. Gloves are useful to collect as they have a habit of getting lost or wet.

Storage areas in outdoor spaces enable children to choose for themselves. Some Forest Schools use a trolley which can be towed to wherever the children are working, and settings might find this a good solution, as it can be wheeled away at the end of the day. Another solution might be storage boxes in a covered area, provided that the outdoor space is secure at night. This saves precious space in sheds, and can be more accessible for children.

Old tyres, planks and crates enable children to shape their own space. Different-sized children will find different-sized resources easier to move around, but social cooperation and rope can move big objects around, so do not underestimate the children. This is getting into the domain of adventure playgrounds, and a visit to one of these can be an illuminating experience.

Equipment – things to save up for

Weatherproof suits for children and possibly for staff will help to change the attitude of the setting to being outdoors in all weathers. It is worth getting the most robust suits you can afford, as it will save money in the long run. Companies such as Mindstretchers (www. mindstretcher.co.uk), Muddypuddles (www.MuddyPuddles.com) and Raindrops (www.raindrops.co.uk) all sell such equipment in small sizes, as do many ship's chandlers. A tip from a practitioner is to buy different sizes in different colours, so that you can identify the sizes quickly.

If you are close enough to water to access a ship's chandler, then you might also locate an old rowing boat that could take the place of your magic carpet. In fact, it can become many things, limited only by the imagination applied to it. Made of wood, it can also become a minibeast habitat over time. Fibreglass is problematic – as it degrades the fibres are a serious hazard, and rain does not drain through it, and in addition it will be unstable if it has a round bottom, so is probably best avoided.

Equipment such as gardening tools and woodworking tools needs to be of good quality. An adult could not efficiently dig soil with a plastic spade, and neither can a child. Blunt tools are much more likely to cause accidents than sharp ones, if only because of the effort required to make them work. Sharp tools will require tuition and trust, but having established ground rules with older children and supervision with younger ones, there is no reason not to use them. Scaled-down versions of most of these are available either from the suppliers mentioned above or from good children's suppliers. If you are going to use potato peelers, look for those with an oval handle rather than a round one, children find them easier to control.

Small equipment, such as mirrors, bug boxes and pooters, can be useful for environmental sessions, but are not strictly Forest School kit. Practitioners find that in Forest School the children need less and less equipment as they become owners of the space, and imaginations take over. Do not feel that a lack of equipment is preventing you from offering Forest School activities. But if you do need specific items then do try asking for sponsorship. Local supermarkets may have charitable budgets that they can use to support good causes, and the Forest Education Initiative wing of the Forestry Commission may have grants, or know of grants, for which you can apply.

Staffing issues – immediate considerations

Managers, owners, head teachers and governors will need to know about the implications of their particular Early Years curricula for outdoor provision. This emphasis on the importance of outdoor experiences is an ideal opportunity to introduce them to the concept of Forest Schools in order to recruit them to the idea of including such activities in their settings. Involving them in sessions for parents is a good way to inform everyone without singling out any particular individual.

Staff may well need training to support a new way of working. This may be a specific Forest School course offered at another site, or it can be an INSET session, sharing knowledge and good practice. An awareness-raising session can be a good start, and gives practitioners a chance to share their concerns as well as their excitement. More confident staff can work alongside less enthusiastic ones to model how to offer minimal intervention and to allow children to make their own decisions. This will help to ensure that staff are sold on the idea that children can learn for themselves outdoors and help them to be positive role models for all aspects of outdoor play. Another way is to facilitate visits to other settings where there is quality outdoor provision and observe children in that environment.

Induction sessions for parents and new staff, and information in handbooks will help to smooth transitions and prevent misunderstandings. The evidence from settings who are engaged in Forest School is that once parents have experienced what is on offer they become enthusiastic supporters, and often volunteers. My own handbook contained the simple statement that children would get dirty at the nursery, so expensive clothes were not suitable. Stated in writing, it gives staff support if parents comment on their children's condition at the end of the day.

Longer-term goals for staff

As a part of continuing professional development for staff, the following knowledge and skills will increase the success of Forest School activities:

- Being actively listening adults.

- Having the courage to let children lead.

- Understanding the importance of giving children time to reflect when they are outdoors.

- Knowing that children could be outdoors all day, every day, throughout the year without anyone being concerned that they are not learning.

- Observation skills.

- First aid and risk assessment training.

Forest School training for key staff will enhance the quality of the activities on offer. It is also worth researching opportunities to visit a nursery working outside in another country, or to observe Forest School-type sessions, to see the children's responses. Local education authorities do sometimes arrange group visits abroad, and there are a few private organisations doing so, too. You will not see Forest School as we are usually offering it in the UK, but it will be interesting and informative.

 Discussion points

In this chapter I have suggested ways in which the ethos of Forest School can be incorporated into the outdoor play of all settings and set out some simple ways of offering all children Forest School-type activities. Hopefully this has given you some ideas that you can discuss with colleagues. Think about the following points:

- What alterations can be made to the outdoor environment immediately?
- What changes could be made to the practice in the setting immediately?
- What are the next three steps to take?

Further reading

Knight, S. (2011c) *Risk and Adventure in Early Years Outdoor Play*. London: Sage.

Ryder Richardson, G. (2006) *Creating a Space to Grow*. London: David Fulton.

Waller, T. (2007) 'The trampoline tree and the swamp monster with 18 heads: outdoor play in the Foundation Stage and Foundation Phase', *Education 3–13*, 35(4): 393–407.

Warden, C. (2005) *The Potential of a Puddle*. Perthshire: Mindstretchers.

Forest School with Other Groups and in Other Countries

Introduction

Throughout this book I have been extolling the virtues of Forest School for children in the Foundation Stage. But if the effects are as valuable and effective as Forest School practitioners claim, then might there not also be benefits in participating in Forest School for other groups? This indeed has been the finding of various groups of practitioners.

In this chapter I will review the value of Forest School as it applies to any group of people at any age. I will use the oldest Forest School sites, those at Bridgwater College and at Burnworthy in Somerset, to illustrate my points. These settings have been offering Forest School to a wide range of participants for approximately 10 years, and the benefits seen there can inform this chapter. I will then go on to look at some other examples of projects springing up in other settings in the UK, which I have investigated in greater depth in Knight (2011a). I will also introduce some of the international developments that are explored in more depth in Knight (2013). Some of these projects are linked to research that will inform the wider educational establishment about Forest School and its benefits. It is only by amassing such an evidence base that Forest School will become more widely adopted.

The universal benefits of Forest School

As stated in Chapter 1, it was a trip to Denmark in 1993 by the early years department at Bridgwater College that started the development of Forest School in the UK. One of the original staff team was a lecturer who supported groups of students at the college who had learning difficulties. So it was inevitable that at the same time that the provision of Forest School was being developed for the college nursery children, it was also being developed for the college students with learning difficulties. This two-pronged development heralded an early recognition that Forest School has wider applications.

In Chapter 4, I list the outcomes identified by Murray and O'Brien from their appraisals of Forest School in Wales in 2005. A re-examination of these demonstrates why Forest School was recognised as being relevant to students with special needs at an early stage. Enabling young people with special needs to develop the skills and abilities listed below matches exactly with the 'Skills for Life' agenda:

- **Confidence**. Increased self-confidence and self-belief, and demonstrating independence.

- **Social skills**. Increased awareness of the consequences of their actions on peers and others, and learning to work cooperatively.

- **Language and communication**. More sophisticated language is prompted by experiences at Forest School.

- **Motivation and concentration**. A keenness to participate and an increased ability to focus on specific tasks.

- **Physical skills**. Improved stamina and gross motor skills through free and easy movement; fine motor skills by making things.

- **Knowledge and understanding**. Increased respect for the environment and an interest in their natural surroundings.

- **New perspectives**. Teachers and others see participants in different settings, which provides another perspective on their characters and abilities.

- **Ripple effects**. Changing the attitudes of parents and carers to Forest School and the environment.

The Forest School team at Bridgwater soon realised that if there were benefits to the very young and to those with special needs, then there were likely to be benefits to others. Many of us can benefit from help with developing our skills in cooperation, teamwork and decision-making. Most of us at some time need support with our self-esteem, confidence and motivation. If you go onto the college website http://www.bridgwater.ac.uk/subject. php?sector=2&subject=223 now, you will find that they offer Forest School training to a range of groups. Within the college they still support the college nursery, the students with learning difficulties, and the students with emotional and behavioural difficulties. For all of these groups there are benefits that can be identified around the skills stated above: cooperation, teamworking, decision-making, self-esteem, confidence and motivation.

Bridgwater's example has inspired others to use their own particular skills and interests to develop other ways in which Forest School can be beneficial. From consideration of some examples of these we gain a wider picture of the value of the Forest School experience.

Examples in action

Many published examples of Forest School work come from the west of England, or from Wales. This is not surprising, as these are the areas where Forest School has been established for the longest period of time. In order to redress this balance, my examples are all taken from the east of England. They are in a rough order by the ages of the participants.

Case study: Dilham Preschool, Norfolk

This rural preschool has an outdoor area on-site which provides Forest School activities at all times. The children attending the preschool are aged between 2 and 4 years, and all are catered for. Practitioners have undertaken Level 1 training and are keen to enable children to connect with their environment. Activities include walking, building with wood, and tool use. A local primary school has a nature reserve that the preschool can use to have a good look at other aspects of the natural environment.

For bigger events the younger siblings are pushed to Forest School in their prams, and their parents are included. Parents think that Forest School is a very good idea as it teaches children about nature through play. A questionnaire after the first session elicited only positive comments. The parents felt that they, too, had learned new things. This setting is a good example of community cooperation, and of making good use of existing resources.

 ## Case study: Lings Wood, Northamptonshire

The following is a report by Jane Shellabear, Family Learning Coordinator, Northampton CC Adult Learning Services.

Lings Wood local nature reserve is a 23-hectare mosaic of habitats within the heart of some of Northampton's more disadvantaged and deprived social housing estates. The proximity to Woodvale Primary School provided a wonderful opportunity for the Wildlife Trust to work in partnership with the school and other agencies to promote a positive focus for the wood.

Throughout the autumn of 2006 a group of Reception/Year 1 children from Woodvale Primary School with their mothers, fathers and even one grandmother, all took part in outdoor learning sessions at their local nature reserve. Together they enjoyed campfires, built shelters, made mud pies and used natural materials and tools to create crafts and mini-beast homes. These practical activities and free-play sessions were led by trained Forest School leaders from the Pre-School Learning Alliance (PLA) and the Wildlife Trust. Diane Hall from the PLA had been successful in securing lottery grant funding to develop Forest School within the early years. She was able to bring considerable experience to

(Continued)

(Continued)

the programme, and has since gone on to develop Forest Schools across the county of Northamptonshire.

This innovative 12-week project was set up by Jane Shellabear, a family learning coordinator from the Adult Learning Service at Northamptonshire County Council, after a chance encounter with the Forest School coordinator for England. Jane secured funding from the Adult Learning Service to run the Family Learning programme for local parents and their children. Woodvale Primary School recruited the parents and children, the PLA and Wildlife Trust provided trained leaders, and Jane supported the parents, having undertaken initial training with the Green Light Trust.

From September to December the families met together at Lings Wood, working both as multi-generational groups and as separate adult–child groups. The family learning coordinator encouraged the adults to observe their child and consider how the children were enjoying learning and playing in the new environment. The parents also assessed the risks in the outdoor environment and worked to provide their child with the freedom to overcome these safely.

'Everyone approached the programme with enthusiasm', said Lings Wood Environmental Centre Manager, 'but remembering how to lose your inhibitions and play hide and seek in the mud takes time to feel comfortable with'. Therefore, this programme has recreated a sustainable connection with nature and will hopefully result in the whole family revisiting Lings Wood and other nature reserves regularly. Indeed, two of the mums have chosen to take their learning to a higher level and have signed up for funding to train as Forest School Leaders to help facilitate the expansion of Forest School across the county.

'I have absolutely *loved* being outdoors and not worrying if I get dirty or not', enthused one of the mums at the end of the programme. Most rewarding of all, though, was the time dedicated to building a harmonious bond between parents and their child, with many special memories to treasure. 'I have particularly enjoyed some one-to-one time with my daughter, as we have a busy, hectic life,' remarked one of the participants.

The work at Lings Wood nature reserve is a good example of how funding for a one-off project can initiate a range of activities. Families spending more time outside and mums training to lead Forest School have a positive effect on the whole community – this time in an urban setting. The recording of the project by the Lings Wood team has added to the body of evidence to demonstrate the value of Forest School.

Case study: Kenninghall Primary School, Norfolk

Sally Rigby originally took her Year 3/4 class out to do Forest School once a week. This proved to be so successful that now she has developed Forest School sessions for everyone in the school, from reception to Year 6. She is a trained practitioner, as are two teaching assistants (TAs) in the school. The school is in a village setting, and has benefited from the LEA support for Forest School training.

The activities started on the school field, but the school is developing a more appropriate area, with parental help. The school ran a parents' Forest School session, and now they are enthusiastic supporters. The parents help raise funds and participate in working parties. In addition, the local community woodland group is supporting the project. In 2000 the school children were involved in planting new woodland within the village which they hope in time to make use of.

The involvement of the whole community demonstrates how one enthusiast can find others of similar mind and engage in a project to benefit all. Community woods, orchards and other growing spaces are good places to look for support for developing Forest School.

 ## Case study: Essex Wildlife Trust

At the Hanningfield Reservoir Nature Reserve, Becky Gibson, Education Officer with the Essex Wildlife Trust, has been running Forest School with secondary-aged pupils from Ramsden Hall Special School. These are boys with moderate learning difficulties and emotional and behavioural issues, and Becky works closely with the pupils and their care staff. After a preliminary session at the school, she runs a block of six weekly sessions with an overnight camping opportunity. These are seen as beneficial for the skills previously associated with Forest School, namely developing self-confidence and self-belief and demonstrating independence, for social skills, for language and communication, and for motivation and concentration. Becky works on increasing their respect for the environment and on developing an interest in their natural surroundings. She has been surprised by how many of the pupils lack coordination and confidence, and work on their physical abilities has been integrated into the sessions.

(Continued)

(Continued)

Further developments at the Hanningfield Reservoir Nature Reserve have included working alongside the Metropolitan Police to provide Forest School activities for their Provision Schools programme. In Colchester, further north in the county, Becky has worked with the Youth Service on a six-week summer programme for 16- to 18-year-olds to achieve ASDAN awards, an alternative to a GCSE. This is in addition to a range of regular environmental activities for children that include Forest School activity days alongside pond-dipping, bird watching, and so on.

This diversity of projects is made possible by having independent and dedicated organisations. Wildlife Trusts and local ranger services are ideally placed to lead Forest School provision for a wider market. Becky is now looking to establish a research project at Hanningfield, adding to the body of knowledge about Forest School.

 ## Case study: Green Light Trust Project, Suffolk

The Green Light Trust (GLT) has a team of qualified staff who deliver Forest School activities and Forest School training courses in the eastern region, at Level 1 and at Level 3. As a charity, GLT seeks out funding to run pilots and training to inspire and support others in developing Forest School. The following is an extract from the report of one such pilot.

> With support from the Mark Leonard Trust, the Green Light Trust set up a six-week pilot programme to deliver Forest School activities to a small group of excluded pupils from a local Pupil Referral Unit. The aims were to offer the pupils a practical experience of learning in the outdoors and a chance to acquire basic woodland skills, and also to enhance the skills of the Green Light leaders in working with excluded pupils and challenging behaviour in the woodland context. The aim was for the pupils to be introduced to the woodland context and to start to explore it through a variety of modelled, tutor-initiated activities as well as their own self-directed learning and play.
>
> The project was set in Frithy Wood, a site of special scientific interest (SSSI). There are no facilities onsite. Pupils travelled from school to the site (approximately eight miles) by minibus. In early sessions a fire was lit and shelter prepared in advance as weather conditions were cold and wet. Hot drinks were prepared by pupils on

arrival. Sessions one and two involved all pupils trying out loppers and saws. Increased motivation and purpose was provided by the coppicing activity in this respect. Using the tools, techniques and knots learned in earlier sessions the pupils applied their skills to making the site more comfortable, by making benches, to varying designs. In session two the pupils coppiced a small section of the woodland led by the Tree Officer from Suffolk County Council. From session three pupils lit the fire and constructed shelters themselves on arrival. Tutors modelled a range of activities, including collecting appropriate wood for the fire, constructing seats, fire sites, saw horse, shelters, anvils, tables, utensils and cooking sticks. Throughout the sessions, the pupils drew on these according to individual preference and worked safely and appropriately with the tools to create a functional woodland site.

Pupils were prompted to recall the key safety rules and risk assessments involved in working in the wood and related to behaviour around the fire at the start of each session. A significant output (and evidence) was the captioning of colour photographs by the pupils to create workbooks. At the end of each session tutors gave pupils brief but positive feedback individually on their behaviour.

As Forest School aims to be pupil-centred and pupil-led, most of the planned activities took place but not necessarily in the sequence planned. Key factors which influenced the sessions were the weather, fluctuating composition of the group, the pupils' behaviour and responses especially around food, and tutor/leader interventions. Although pupil numbers were small this had the benefit of allowing tutors to build relationships with the pupils and address the need for coping strategies linked to the frequent behavioural issues which emerged during each session.

Pupils responded well to instinctive and familiar activities, such as preparing drinks and sustaining the fire. Tutor-modelled activities, such as wood collection and tool use, were taken up by all pupils as their mood, ability or inclination permitted. Little interest was shown in activities which were not given sufficient introduction, were insufficiently modelled or were perceived as too challenging.

Both tutors have gained enormously from the experience of working with these excluded pupils. It provided an intensive training and learning experience, and enabled them to draw on their training and experience with other groups to see what actually worked in practice with this quite unpredictable and challenging client group. They were particularly pleased that most of the pupils did create and caption a logbook of their Forest School experiences. There is good potential for this activity

(Continued)

(Continued)

to be extended with future client groups, partly in support of those who may be averse to writing in more formal contexts. More significantly this photo-based book with captions written and typed by the pupils can serve as evidence for the OCN Level 1 qualification. The timescale provided by a 10-week Forest School programme would allow them to support and encourage pupils to create files that could be submitted and marked for the OCN Level 1 Forest School Activities Award.

The reports from projects such as this are useful data to add to the range of Forest School applications. Training organisations such as the Green Light Trust are well placed to initiate such projects which additionally contribute to the continuing professional development of the trainers. Recorded pilots can inspire future developments by others.

 ## Case study: Norfolk Broads Authority

Russell Wilson has a range of projects running to support youngsters between the ages of 14 and 19. Three examples give the flavour of his work:

1   NR5 Project: a one-year project for 14- to 16-year-olds developing 'hard' skills around woodland construction and conservation, and 'soft' skills such as communication and teamworking.

2   YMCA Entry to Employment scheme: an eight-week rolling programme for 16- to 19-year-olds.

3   Framlingham Earl School: a partnership project with Norfolk police service for 14- to 16-year-olds, similar to the Essex project mentioned above.

This is a good example of a local authority providing a service to a wide range of users, and on a wide range of sites.

 ## Case study: SEEVIC College, Essex

This large college is in Benfleet and serves a wide area of southern Essex from Southend to the edges of Greater London. It caters mainly for

16- to 18-year-olds on full-time courses, but has a significant number of students over 19 on part-time courses. The students participating in sessions following the Forest School ethos all have moderate learning difficulties (MLD), and a significant proportion are on the autistic spectrum. Their tutor, Kevin Burrows, is researching the effects of the sessions on those students who are on the autistic spectrum as a part of his PhD studies. He is a trained Forest School practitioner.

The wooded area used by the students is on the college campus, and is small. The tutor negotiates access with the ground staff. At present he is not permitted to light fires, but has established a circle of seating logs with a stone-and-willow replica fire to act as a focal point for the group. Around this are three or four small glades linked by short paths, one of which contains the beginnings of a willow structure designed to provide an alternative focal point as well as some shelter. Shelter is an important issue as some of the students move slowly and feel the cold easily. Kevin has obtained a Forestry Commission grant which has paid for robust wellingtons, overalls and overcoats in sufficient numbers for staff and students.

The sessions start and finish in the circle area. Students initially discuss what they will be working on that week. Their activities are linked to their indoor studies with this tutor. These are entry-level courses in performing arts, arts and crafts, and media, and 'Skills for Life' programmes in literacy and numeracy. This wide brief enables Kevin to encourage the students to work in groups on a range of creative tasks.

Kevin has recorded improvements in communication and cooperation, skills that many of these students struggle with (Burrows, in Knight, 2011a: 162). In addition, their creativity is finding outlets that are individual, enabling them to explore their own unique ways of illustrating and communicating their ideas and perspectives. The sessions have been running for several terms now, and are making a significant contribution to the college provision for students with MLD.

Capturing the data from different sessions and using them as the foundation for research will deepen our understanding of why Forest School is such a powerful tool, and lend weight to arguments that all children and many adults would benefit from access to Forest School or similar nature-based experiences.

International developments

Forest School started in the Scandinavian countries, and continues to flourish there (Moser and Martinsen, 2010). It has not only sparked the UK Forest School movement, but also developments in other European countries such as the Czech Republic (Kubala, 2002). Combine this with the spread from Germany of the similar tradition of Wandekinder (Becker et al., 2012), and there is a growing recognition of the importance of wilder outdoor play in the early years in Europe.

In North America the twin impacts of Forest School (particularly in Canada) and of the Children and Nature movement started by Richard Louv's book (Louv, 2010) are creating pressures to enable children to access wilder spaces to promote healthy development. In Australia, too, there is a growing interest in providing wilder outdoor experiences at an early age (Davis et al., 2006). These post-industrial countries wrestle with issues around risk in the same ways as the UK (for example, Little, 2006), with academics and practitioners arguing for managed risk to facilitate learning.

In other countries, the twin pressures seem more likely to be developmental and environmental. Education for sustainable development is a key driver, as can be seen in the contributions to *International Perspectives on Forest School* (Knight, 2013). This is the idea that by engaging children emotionally and socially in their environment from an early age, they will grow up to love and care for the planet in a holistic way. For example, an international student of mine recently introduced me to Korean 'Sangtae Kindergarten', where children are involved in growing and preparing food using traditional methods, stating that 'the nature field is also where children learn about plants' ecosystems'.

Whether the initial impetus comes from a concern about the health and well-being of young children, or about the future health and well-being of the planet, it would appear that across the world there is a wave of interest in providing wilder and play-based experiences for our youngest children. In this way we seem to be attempting to reconnect future generations with the lands they live in, which can only be to the benefit of both.

Conclusion

This is a small sample of the many ways in which Forest School is being used to benefit children, young people and communities. They demonstrate that the idea of Forest School has grown and developed, and is being used in creative and novel ways. It is true that those who have been involved longest sometimes worry about preserving the ethos of the original idea, but equally, most are excited about the possibilities inherent in developing the idea. It is to be hoped that the National Forest School Association will continue the discussion about how to preserve the ethos and promote the development of the idea without those two strands coming into conflict. In the meantime, it is up to practitioners and enthusiasts to explore how they can best use the idea encapsulated in the term 'Forest School'.

Discussion points

This chapter has considered the relevance of Forest School to groups other than the Foundation Stage. I have described how the ethos has benefits for adults, and for children and young people of all ages. There is a list of different projects showing how these benefits have been provided in different places and by very different groups of people. In the previous chapter I asked practitioners to consider how to provide the benefits of Forest School activities for all the children in their setting, even if they cannot access a complete series of Forest School sessions. In this chapter I suggest that readers speculate about which groups known to them would benefit from Forest School sessions, and how that might be accomplished:

- Are there any groups of people or individuals linked to your settings who would benefit from Forest School sessions?
- What might help them to access Forest School?
- How could you help them to find their way to Forest School?
- What might hinder them from accessing Forest School?
- How could you help them to remove the obstacles to Forest School?

Further reading

Bunting, C. (2006) *Interdisciplinary Teaching Through Outdoor Education.* Champaign, IL: Human Kinetics.
Hope, G., Austin, R., Dismore, H., Hammond, S. and Whyte, T. (2007) 'Wild woods or urban jungle: playing it safe or freedom to roam', *Education 3–13*, 35(4): 321–32.
Knight, S. (ed.) (2011a) *Forest School for All.* London: Sage.
Knight, S. (ed.) (2013) *International Perspectives on Forest School.* London: Sage.

9

Outcomes from Forest School Participation – Some Research

Chapter objectives

- To describe some of the published research relating to Forest School.
- To describe some of the research undertaken by the author.
- To evaluate these projects.
- To consider the direction of travel in research around Forest School.

Introduction

When this book was first published there had been very little research published in this country regarding the effects of Forest School on the participants. There had been two NEF/FEI studies (Murray, 2004; Murray and O'Brien, 2005), both commissioned by the Forestry Commission on established Forest School provision, and a replication of their study methods in Scotland (Borradaile, 2006). Those studies looked at the immediate effects of Forest School on the children taking part.

Following on from this, I replicated the last NEF/FEI study (Murray and O'Brien, 2005) at Nayland School in Suffolk, enabling me to contrast their data with mine to establish some new ideas about Forest School research. I will describe this work in the first part of this chapter.

I also considered the problems of trying to identify the long-term effects of experiencing Forest School in the Foundation Stage. I tried to design a longitudinal study to examine the long-term effects of a Forest School experience in the Foundation Stage, including data from Nayland School and All Saints School, Lawshall. I collected data from children from each year group, and from their parents, and talked to the teachers who have not been involved in Forest School but have encountered children after they have had that experience. This study is described in the second part of this chapter.

This raised an interesting issue about the differences in the groups I looked at in comparison with previous studies. The two NEF/FEI studies and the Scottish study focused largely on schools and nurseries where the funding to attend Forest School has been available because they have been identified as being in need. Nayland and Lawshall are rural schools with a catchment that is largely economically secure and such funding is therefore unlikely to exist – another key difference between the other studies and this. Both have a long association with Forest School, the Green Light Trust and environmental education. This demonstrates that the impact of Forest School is different where the need is different, but that Forest School is equally important in the outcomes for young children.

The NEF/FEI studies

The New Economics Foundation (NEF) is an independent organisation which works with other bodies to research social issues and support proposals for change. They develop innovative ways to measure outcomes with the intention of providing practitioners with new perspectives on their work. In 2004 the NEF published their study *Forest School Evaluation Project: A Study in Wales*, a participative study of two Welsh pilot projects, funded by the Forestry Commission. Wales was the first region to achieve significant funding for their Forest Schools, from various arms of local and regional government, to support schools identified as 'being in need of support for community development' (Murray, 2004: 7).

In 2005 the same group published a further study, applying the techniques developed in the first study to various English Forest School settings (Murray and O'Brien, 2005: 16–17). In this instance all the groups were in the Foundation Stage or Key Stage 1, again attending

Forest Schools a bus ride away run by Forest School leaders hitherto unknown to the children. And again, the data analysis was initially done with or by the participants, and the later work done by Richard Murray, this time in partnership with Liz O'Brien from Forest Research (an arm of the Forestry Commission). The published outcomes of the study included a 'Forest School Self-Appraisal Toolkit'. This is made up of instructions for use, templates and guidance for what to do with the information gathered (Murray and O'Brien, 2005: Appendix 7). Below is an account of how I used this at Nayland School in order to replicate their study.

These studies concentrated on eight outcomes identified by NEF in discussion with the Forest School providers with whom they were working. They were as follows:

1 **Confidence**. Increased self-confidence and self-belief from freedom, time and space, to learn, grow and demonstrate independence.

2 **Social skills**. Increased awareness of the consequences of their actions on other people, peers and adults, and learning to work cooperatively.

3 **Language and communication**. More sophisticated written and spoken language prompted by children's sensory experiences at Forest School.

4 **Motivation and concentration**. A keenness to participate in exploratory learning and play activities, an ability to focus on specific tasks for extended periods of time.

5 **Physical skills**. Improved stamina and gross motor skills through free and easy movement; fine motor skills by making things.

6 **Knowledge and understanding**. Increased respect for the environment, interest in natural surroundings; observational improvements – identify flora and fauna and changing seasons, and so on.

7 **New perspectives**. Teachers and other adults see children in different settings, which improves their understanding and helps identify learning styles.

8 **Ripple effects**. Asking to go out at weekends and holidays, parents' interests and attitudes to Forest School and environment are changing.

I chose to focus on the same outcomes in order to produce comparable data.

Storyboarding at Nayland

The first part of the Self-Appraisal Toolkit is a participative story-boarding exercise to establish the individual propositions of the particular Forest School. Murray and O'Brien suggest eight interlinking questions, with prompts to stimulate discussion (Murray and O'Brien, 2005: Appendix 7.1). This then was my starting point with the Foundation Stage staff at Nayland School.

The block of Forest School sessions that I was planning to use for my study was in Spring 2007, starting on 31 January, and running for six weeks. On 22 January I arranged a meeting with the two Foundation Stage teachers to look at the storyboard questions. First we brainstormed, and then we discussed and refined our answers. This covered steps one and two suggested by Murray and O'Brien. Below are the questions asked, and the answers we arrived at.

Question 1: describe the world in terms of the need that this Forest School is addressing.

1 Having the bigger space to learn in – especially important for the kinaesthetic learners.

2 The effects on the self-esteem of the youngest children in the school.

3 Seeing different aspects of the children from those portrayed in school – even in the outdoor area – gives a different knowledge of the children.

4 Developing a sense of awe and wonder, and fostering a caring attitude for the natural world around them.

5 Changing modern attitudes about looking after and taking care, and developing a sense of personal responsibility.

Question 2: what are the key elements of the Forest School ethos for the success of this particular setting?

1 The enthusiasm and commitment of the staff – teachers and TAs.

2 Staffing with higher ratios than in class.

3 Parents being on board – in the four years it has run, only one has been irreversibly overprotective. New parents are aware both

through word of mouth and through Forest School being sold as a part of the school's offering.

4 Wood on site – eases toileting issues, setting-up times, and so on.

Question 3: what effects do you expect to see straight away?

1 Children taking control – developing independence and resource-fulness.

2 Their understanding of boundaries and danger becomes explicit, making it easier to assess and progress.

3 Collaboration – including a mixing up of groups in unpredictable ways.

Question 4: what effects and changes do you expect to see in the future?

1 There are children who grow in confidence.

2 There are children who grow in self-esteem.

3 The collaborative skills and teamwork transfer into the school environment.

4 Children recognise the importance of collaborative skills and teamwork.

Question 5: where possible, describe the longer term or wider changes for people involved in Forest School that (a) your Forest School will be wholly responsible for, and (b) your project may contribute to.

For the majority, the skills would have developed anyway, but slower, but for one or two children, Forest School will be the key to develop-ing self-confidence, self-esteem, and/or collaborative skills. Forest School does different and unique things to relationships.

Question 6: for every immediate effect identified in question 3 above, ask 'so what?' or 'why is that important? (This links to a new initiative within the school's cluster group to use 'Building Learning Power' (BLP) by Guy Claxton.)

1 Being a lifelong learner – the skills that say that learning is forever, there will not always be someone to help, so go and find it out for yourself.

2 Seeing first hand the children's conceptual understanding of danger for themselves and others. Helps teaching about safety in a practical way that is real and has a purpose.

3 Links to lifelong training, listening to others, working out who can help, recognising the skills of others.

Question 7: for every effect and change identified in question 4 above, ask 'so what?' or 'why is that important?

1 Will be better learners, which can only happen if they believe in themselves.

2 Meets an expectation of the school, therefore affects them through out the school and for the future.

Question 8: what barriers do you foresee that could prevent any of this happening?

1 Exhaustion of staff – resilience is lowered and therefore teachers are less able to cope with rubbish, fly-tipping, and so on.

2 Staffing – TA support relies on goodwill. Parents will occasionally do an odd session, but no commitment to their own participation.

3 Whole-school commitments over time, such as site degradation, equipment (tools, blankets, and so on) and communication with ground staff.

It was an interesting process to go through, as we had not had this discussion in the four years we have been working on this project. This self-appraisal gave greater clarity to our thoughts and to our communications with others. In addition, what came out of it was a deeper understanding of our perspectives on the eight specific outcomes.

Discussion on the eight outcomes of Forest School identified by NEF

1 **Confidence**. *Increased self-confidence and self-belief from freedom, time and space, to learn, grow and demonstrate independence.*

   What sets Forest School apart is attendance on a regular basis over time – some take time to become familiar and confident with Forest School and the associated routines. They develop ownership, encouraging relaxation and comfortableness with it, and a relationship with their woodland setting at their own pace. Embedded routines provide stability, consistency and security. Knowing boundaries leaves freedom for thought and activities. Freedom to take risks that are managed, gives independence and a desire to explore further. Child-led learning in a setting flexible enough to adapt to their interests allows them to make their own discoveries and construct their own learning.

2 **Social skills**. *Increased awareness of the consequences of their actions on other people, peers and adults, and to work cooperatively.*

   It is about encouraging children to identify their own strengths and recognise the value they bring to relationships, not about creating a class of charismatic leaders. Thus they learn to value the contribution of others. Pro-social behaviour such as giving, helping, sharing, and comforting are encouraged.

3 **Language and communication**. *More sophisticated written and spoken language prompted by children's sensory experiences at Forest School.*

   Opportunities to convey messages, express feelings and make social contact, turn-taking, negotiation, listening to others, talking about Forest School in class and at home. Increased and developed use of language, and improved vocabulary through spontaneous talk and descriptive language. Enthusiasm inspires new words and greater fluency. Communication and self-confidence are linked – increased willingness to communicate is an indicator of greater confidence. Inspiration to learn new words, create imaginary play and make up stories and ideas comes from their surroundings.

4 **Motivation and concentration**. *A keenness to participate in exploratory learning and play activities; an ability to focus on specific tasks for extended periods of time.*

Children's interests motivate their desire to learn – outdoor environments tend to fascinate, thus stimulating their innate curiosity. Child-initiated learning enables practitioners to see what intrigues the children, who can then work, solve problems, and discover new things, ideas and concepts. Wonderment and awe was an expression used in the National Curriculum – it happens naturally by being close to nature. Learning about the environment and using imagination when they discover new phenomena, and create places for them in their world.

5 **Physical skills**. *Improved stamina and gross motor skills through free and easy movement; fine motor skills by making things.*

Children are helped, tested and challenged at Forest School, improving their range and quality of movement. Gaining stamina may be a combination of walking to Forest School and the exercise of a whole session. Confidence to undertake risks and challenges comes through learning how to do things safely, and through exploring boundaries – maybe through visiting new areas of their wood. Space and opportunity to learn and experiment through the amount of space available, and the tactile experiences including different weather conditions. As they gain in experience they trip over less often, and cope with putting on protective clothing more easily.

6 **Knowledge and understanding**. *Increased respect for the environment, interest in natural surroundings; observational improvements – identify flora and fauna and changing seasons, and so on.*

This may be a different environment or a familiar one approached differently. Curiosity developed in the wood transfers to the world beyond Forest School, increasing the desire to learn and explore. Knowledge is inspired by child-initiated exploration and supplied by the expertise of the practitioner. Understanding develops over weeks of repetitions that increases their awareness of the impact of their actions. Ownership also develops over time, giving a degree of pride and confidence.

7 **New perspectives**. *Teachers and other adults see children in different settings, which improves their understanding and helps identify learning styles.*

This facilitates a more positive relationship between child and practitioner, and a holistic view of their unique strengths and skills.

8 **Ripple effects**. *Asking to go out at weekends and holidays, parents' interests and attitudes to Forest School and environment are changing.*

Open days and celebrations can help allay worries about risks, exposure to inclement weather and the process of learning. This ripples into the wider community. Evidence of skills transferred to other settings include an interest in the environment, plus all manner of strengths that aid success in formal learning.

The next step, to decide how we would know that the Forest School experience was a success, was for us summarised in our answers to questions 3–7. We did not feel the need to make it more explicit by drawing up a poster, as directed by the toolkit. Exploring why this was the case gave me two answers. One was that the questions prompt each other, and the success criteria are therefore explicit in the answers to questions 3 and 4. This is a part of the research design. In the first of the pilot studies the outcomes proposed and affirmed (Murray, 2004: 24) identified the criteria that would make Forest School a sustainable reality for the pilot settings. This is a really worthwhile outcome for a new setting, but at Nayland we have passed that point, as Forest School is a sustainable reality.

Recording sessions

The NEF Self-Appraisal Toolkit provides three templates for recording sessions. However, they do say:

> With the focus on self-appraisal, this means that it is the people involved in each project – the evaluating practitioners themselves – who must decide what are for them the most appropriate and convenient ways to record systematically the changes they see taking place before them (Murray and O'Brien, 2005: Appendix 7.2).

The first template provided is an introductory sheet for each Forest School session, which I did complete at the start of each session. As the semi-outsider in the group it gave me some time for reflection about the sessions, but did not generate useful information about particular children. The school staff did not engage with this form at all, finding it duplicated existing records.

I also elected to undertake a narrative observation of each session. However, it is extremely time-consuming, and really only practical when you are supernumerary, as I was. Even then, and even for an experienced observer like myself, with over 20 years of nursery observations in my pocket, it is fraught with limitations, and the children would have preferred my company – see below:

Diary extract:

Child E3 spent some time squeezing mud onto a stick. She massaged it with a dreamy expression, and asked me 'Do you want to feel it? It's all squidgy'. I did so, then handed it back. She carried on working the mud, and soon after she asked me 'Do you want another squish?' but I declined, and she moved away . . .

Children E3 and E2 had noticed that my hands were dirty and offered to clean them. I put my notebook away, and they took a hand each, wiping them with leaves. 'Now you can't write any notes,' they said, triumphantly.

I also started by using a pocket tape recorder. In the past I have obtained rich data using such a device inside nursery settings, and I had permission to use such a device from the staff to enrich my data collection. The advantages of taping include being able to replay a sequence of utterances the better to understand it. The disadvantages include the practicalities of multiple voices and background noise, considerably greater outdoors than in, and in the time needed to transcribe the material. I was forced to abandon this method after Week 3, but the material I collected up to that point was very rich.

At the end of each week, after discussions with the staff, I reflected on how the six specific outcomes had been evidenced that week. This enabled me to evaluate all the data collected that week, through observations by the staff, by myself, by the tape recordings, and from discussions of the reporting template, against those six criteria.

Reflection poster

The third and final part of the NEF Self-Appraisal Toolkit process is to create an evaluation poster in a workshop session with all the adult participants. This exercise purports to offer a way to evaluate the highs and lows of the block of sessions, to review the original goals set, and to set 'future targets, goals and outcomes' (Murray and O'Brien, 2005: Appendix 7).

The staff and I met in the week after the sessions were finished. We reflected back on the storyboard, as directed, and agreed that our outcomes had been met. We discussed the fact that the school council has requested that all classes should have Forest School, and that the Year 1 class will be doing sessions in the summer term of 2007. This has implications for site degradation, staffing, and curriculum linking, none of which are insoluble, but all of which require careful consideration.

Evaluation of NEF study replication

My findings do replicate the findings of the NEF study, when looking at the eight specific outcomes identified. With respect to the first six outcomes I considered in my replication of the NEF/FEI studies, I have taken statements from all three studies to demonstrate their similarities, see Table 9.1.

Table 9.1   Comparisons between studies

		Study in Wales (Murray, 2004: 22)	Study in England (Murray and O'Brien, 2005: 32)	Nayland School study, 2007 (diary extracts)
1	Self-esteem and self-confidence	Allows freedom to wander in a new environment to build confidence in the exploration of the unknown	Comes from children having the freedom and the time and space to learn, grow and demonstrate their independence	Organising collecting poles for tipi (confidence), articulating new ideas (independence)
2	Cooperation and awareness of others (social skills)	Good for a whole-class approach as it helps a class to 'gel'	Sharing, cooperative play, awareness of consequences of actions	Reinstating base camp, collaborative play, relationship with adults
3	Motivation and attitudes to learning	Encourages children to question and explore	Keenness to participate, concentration span, positive attitude	Perseverance to make fishing lines, concentration on games and stick-peeling

		Study in Wales (Murray, 2004: 22)	Study in England (Murray and O'Brien, 2005: 32)	Nayland School study, 2007 (diary extracts)
4	Ownership and pride in local environment	Established patterns of behaviour, parents and carers invited in	Covered in 6 below	Anger at changes in 'our' camp, wormery to protect worms, discussions and action about base camp
5	Improved relationship with and understanding of outdoors	Routines in the woods, discovery of new and unfamiliar aspects of environment	Covered in 6 below	Remembering rules, observing crows return, seeing newt, fungus, and so on.
6	Skills and knowledge levels	Observe individuals' development and understanding	Respect for environment interest in surroundings, observations	Child 1 on upside-down snail, child 2 on birdsong, child 3 on crows nests, child 4 spots violets

What we saw in Nayland were the same effects that were seen in Wales and in the 2005 English study. The findings are therefore replicable, and in a setting quite unlike the previous studies, giving this methodology credibility as a useful tool. What it does not do is to say anything about the longevity of the effects of Forest School on young children. Murray and O'Brien (2005: 79) identify this as a recommendation, and as an issue in need of thorough assessment.

Long-term effects, and whether they are measurable

I decided to take up the challenge of attempting to record the long-term effects of Forest School in the second part of my study. I used a questionnaire as my principal method, to ask parents whether they thought that Forest School had made a difference over time, and then to ask the children whether they thought that Forest School had made a difference over time. A questionnaire (if successful) can be used repeatedly, and thus, if my study was successful, I would have created a methodological tool to reuse in other settings in order to add to the body of research.

I asked the parents rather than the teachers for two reasons. One was that it gave me a bigger sample size, and looked at the level of the individual child rather than at the level of a class, where individual differences might get lost. The other was that parents know their children best, have their best interests at heart and are more likely to notice those aspects of development covered by the specific learning outcomes. Involving parents also raised their awareness of the research, and helps get them on board as a pressure group. I did, however, discuss the impact of Forest School with the staff in an informal manner. I asked the children because they are the biggest stakeholders in the process, and have an interest in the development of Forest School. I opted to visit each class and discuss the questions, then take a vote on the answers, which I then recorded.

Going into the classes also allowed me to explain what I was doing, a part of the ethical dimension of this study. I had permission from the school and parents for the whole project and I had explained the purpose of the questionnaire to the parents, and all the material for this part of the study is numerical (apart from parents' additional comments) and anonymous, but I still felt that the children should know why I was asking the questions and how the data would be used.

The questionnaires

The questionnaires were an attempt to address the issues but are open to criticism. They were based on the questions asked in the study above, and as a result are more 'leading' in nature than I would prefer. However, given the paucity of data in the field, I include them here for consideration. They are supported by 'school gate' discussions and the conversations that they stimulated with the children. Hopefully, others will follow with different methodologies.

Carrying out the study

I piloted the questionnaire (Figure 9.1) at Lawshall School in Suffolk with their Year 1 class. I felt that this would give me a similar response to the Nayland parents, as the school is another rural Suffolk school, and of a similar size.

The response from the Nayland parents was 19 out of 100, less than 20 per cent, just below the average return rate for such questionnaires, and I suspect that the return rate from parents dropped off as their children grew older. Four parents elected to respond to the opportunity by making a statement about Forest School rather than complete the numerical scores, but all their comments were very positive. This left 15 to score. I considered the low response rate and identified three possible reasons. One is that Forest School is an established part of the school, so parents might not have felt that there was anything to be gained for their children by responding. Another is that the links between home and school are strong at Nayland, and parents had just been closely involved with the introduction of 'Building Learning Power' (Claxton, 2002), so might have felt a sense of overload. Third, my instructions were not as clear as they should have been, so perhaps the teachers distributing the questionnaires did not imbue them with any sense of urgency. Whatever the reasons, anecdotal 'school gate' feelings towards Forest School are positive, and I am not concerned for the school by the low response rate.

After receiving the responses, I went in to the school to carry out the oral questionnaire (Figure 9.2) with the children. It was interesting to note the actual loss from the sample, one of the problems noted above. In the Year 1 class all 25 children had attended Forest School. In Year 2 there were 6 who did not out of 24, giving 18 who did. In Year 3 there were 22 children, 18 who did and 4 who did not. But in Year 4 only 7 out of 20 experienced Forest School because they are the younger children, and we had not started in time for the oldest in the class. Therefore, looking at the two middle classes, there is a loss of about 25 only two years after the Forest School sessions in the Foundation Stage, and one could predict with some certainty that this figure would rise over time.

The children were enthusiastic, and the discussions that the sessions enabled prompted fond reminiscences, and tales to those who had not been there. Indeed, the school council has requested that all classes have Forest School sessions, and the logistics of this are under consideration. I found it was only practicable to score the votes as 0, 1, 3 and 5.

To parents: please circle the number that best describes your answer.
5 is high (a big effect), 0 is low (no effect).

As a result of their Forest School experience do you think that your child:

1. Is more self-confident?	5	4	3	2	1	0
2. Is more independent?	5	4	3	2	1	0
3. Has a more enquiring and exploratory attitude to learning in and out of school?	5	4	3	2	1	0
4. Has a more relaxed attitude to new experiences?	5	4	3	2	1	0
5. Is better at playing with others?	5	4	3	2	1	0
6. Listens better to adults and children?	5	4	3	2	1	0
7. Knows what they themselves are good at?	5	4	3	2	1	0
8. Has a more positive attitude to life?	5	4	3	2	1	0
9. Has a wider vocabulary?	5	4	3	2	1	0
10. Is more prepared to discuss things of interest?	5	4	3	2	1	0
11. Listens to others more?	5	4	3	2	1	0
12. Plays more imaginatively?	5	4	3	2	1	0
13. Can concentrate better?	5	4	3	2	1	0
14. Is more motivated to learn?	5	4	3	2	1	0
15. Has a greater awareness of the world around them?	5	4	3	2	1	0
16. Is better at problem solving?	5	4	3	2	1	0
17. Has greater stamina?	5	4	3	2	1	0
18. Is more physically able?	5	4	3	2	1	0
19. Is happier to challenge themselves physically?	5	4	3	2	1	0
20. Has improved dexterity?	5	4	3	2	1	0
21. Has an increased respect for the environment?	5	4	3	2	1	0
22. Is keen to find out more about things of interest to them?	5	4	3	2	1	0
23. Observes changes in their surroundings more quickly?	5	4	3	2	1	0
24. Is quicker to see connections between their actions and the consequences of them?	5	4	3	2	1	0

Please state any benefits that your child gained that have not been listed above:

Figure 9.1   Parent questionnaire

<u>Oral questionnaire for children:</u>
(5 is a big effect, 0 is no effect)

1. Confidence

   How many of you think that doing Forest School has affected how confident you are in school?

   5   4   3   2   1   0

2. Social skills

   How many of you think that doing Forest School has affected how good you are at working with other people?

   5   4   3   2   1   0

3. Communication

   How many new words did you learn while doing Forest School (descriptive as well as factual)?

   5   4   3   2   1   0

4. Motivation and concentration

   Did doing Forest School make it easier to concentrate on other lessons back in school?

   5   4   3   2   1   0

5. Physical skills

   How many of you think that doing Forest School has affected how good you are at physical skills?

   5   4   3   2   1   0

6. Knowledge and understanding

   How many of you think that doing Forest School has increased how much you know about the environment?

   5   4   3   2   1   0

7. New perspectives

   How many of you think that doing Forest School helped you to get to know the staff better?

   5   4   3   2   1   0

8. Ripple effects

   Now that you have done Forest School, do you persuade your parents to take you out into the environment more often?

   5   4   3   2   1   0

Figure 9.2 Oral questionnaire for children

Photocopiable:
Forest School and Outdoor Learning in the Early Years, 2nd Edition, SAGE Publications © Sara Knight, 2013

Results

The graphs in Figure 9.3 compare the data between the groups by question, showing the differences between the two adult groups and the children. As the children's data is only for ratings 0, 1, 3 and 5, the comparisons are not straightforward, but they do show interesting trends. As a generalisation, I think I can state that the results are positive. For almost all the questions in almost all the groups, the majority of respondents have rated the questions with a score of 3 (halfway) or above.

Looking at the Lawshall data, there is a clear peak of ratings at level 4, with rating level 3 a close second. Rating 5 is significantly higher than ratings 1, 2 or no score. This indicates that parents consider Forest School makes a positive contribution to their children's educational experience. But these are all parents whose children experienced Forest School recently. The Nayland data is spread between children who experienced Forest School recently, and children who experienced Forest School up to four years ago.

It is interesting that the Nayland data shows the same curve, but with lower scores. The Lawshall data tops 60 per cent for question 6, whereas the Nayland data peaks at 46.6 per cent for the same question. While the results are still positive, this could indicate a falling-off of the recognition of the effects over time. This is completely different to the children's responses, where the oldest children are the most enthusiastic. This could be because the group was so much smaller than the other classes, or because there is a nostalgia effect.

There were a higher number of 'don't knows' among the children than among the parents. This is not surprising as the parents had time to reflect on their answers, while the children were asked to respond on the spot. I tried to strike a balance between giving them time to discuss before voting and keeping the momentum up to keep their interest, but I suspect that for some the thinking time was insufficient.

On comparing the data between groups it is clear that the children are more unambiguously enthusiastic than the parents. This reflects the request the school council is making to give all children Forest School experiences every year. As Bilton states 'outdoors is a preferred place for boys' (2003: 76) and 'children have different learning styles; these can be visual, auditory and kinaesthetic . . . schools tend to put a heavy stress on the other two styles' (2003: 72), that is, not the kinaesthetic experience more easily accessed outside. The children

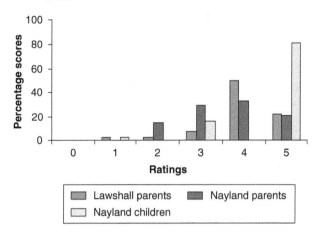

Question 1 – increased confidence and self-esteem

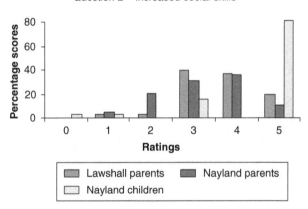

Question 2 – increased social skills

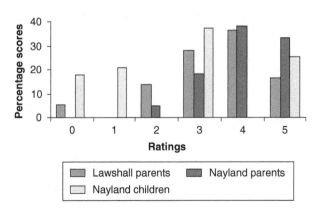

Question 3 – improved language and communication skills

(Continued)

Figure 9.3   (Continued)

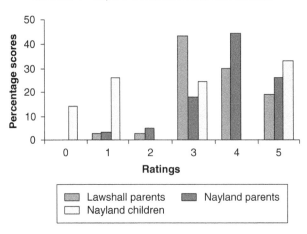

Question 4 – improved motivation and concentration

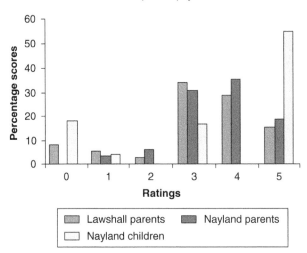

Question 5 – improved physical skills

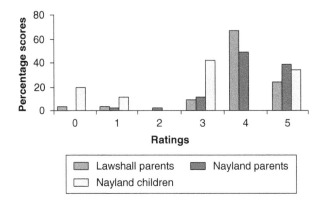

Question 6 – increased environmental knowledge and understanding

Figure 9.3   Comparison tables for questions 1–6

here are voting clearly for an educational experience that enables these needs to be met.

The children's lowest rating was for question 3, about improved language and communication skills, the highest percentage being 36.8 per cent for level 3 and 25 per cent for level 5. This could be the way in which I asked the question, or their failure to recognise a truth. Certainly looking at the records you can see an incredibly rich linguistic experience which I commented on in Chapter 6. This score is similar to the parents', who gave most questions a similar score. Their next lowest score is for question 4, on improved motivation, where only 33.8 per cent rated the question at level 5 and 25 per cent at level 3. This was a question where Foundation Stage teachers had reported a marked improvement in children for whom this is an issue. I suspect that it is also a factor that children would find hard to recognise in themselves, although it attracts comparatively high scores from both sets of parents.

Other comparisons between the responses to different questions show all three groups scoring question 6 highly. This could be said to be predictable, in that the knowledge and understanding that the children gain about the environment is the most obvious outcome of Forest School. For example, there were examples of discovering a new fungus, observing the signs of the coming of spring, and recounting the locomotion of a worm.

The children were the only group to be asked questions 7 and 8. The results of this questioning are given here. Question 7 was about the perception of the children by the adults and vice versa, and how Forest School enables the development of their relationships. 60.3 per cent of the children gave this the highest score, which is a strong indicator that children value this opportunity to get to know staff differently. In the answer the staff give to the second storyboard question (see Figure 9.3) this is clearly an element that they value (see Chapter 6).

For question 8 about the ripple effects of Forest School into the wider community, 54.4 per cent of children felt that it had made a difference to the amount of time that they spent outside with their families. As this is a rural school where many of the parents are often professionals who are likely to spend time with their children at weekends, I felt that this was a high figure. It may represent wishful thinking about Forest School on the part of the children, but as a perception it is an interesting one.

New Research

Following on from this work, other academics have continued with explorations that relate to Forest School. For example, O'Brien and Murray (2007) have summarised the work outlined above, and the Forestry Commission in Scotland have continued to fund research (Lovell, 2008; Roe et al., 2008). This solid underpinning has been very useful in supporting the development of Forest School in Scotland and Wales, where the regional governments have been financially supportive to Forest School. Also of interest are three new threads of thought, not always from academics and researchers directly involved with Forest School, but highlighting areas that impact and have meaning in the Forest School context.

The first of these comes from the discipline of social geography, where academics such as Kraftl et al. (2012) consider the impact of geographical spaces on children, considering how ownership and agency increase commitment, growth and learning. A sense of space has been commented on as being important to young children by many professionals, in terms of developing their sense of identity, community and responsibility to the environment. The work above ties in with that of Wattchow and Brown (2011), who have written about how different forms of outdoor education carry a shape determined by the environment they inhabit. This in turn can affect attitudes to that education, and therefore to the outcomes of that education for participants, in the long term as well as the short term. These authors are largely considering outcomes for older children and young adults, but when you take into consideration Tim Waller's 2007 paper discussing how young children relate to spaces and identify them, it is clear that 'owning' a wilder space impacts on children's well-being and sense of belonging. Space, ownership and sustainability are ripe for further research.

The second thread of thought emerged clearly at the conference 'Philosophical Perspectives in Outdoor Education' at the University of Edinburgh in May 2012. Of particular interest was the paper by Mark Leather (2012), which seeks to explore the relationship between social constructivism and Forest School. His discussion relates directly to working with young children and, as such, ties in with the work on social pedagogy in early outdoor education, expounded in Becker et al. (2012). Further exploration of the philosophical perspectives of Forest School pedagogy is a clear need, and is on the agenda for the National Forest School Association.

Finally, and leading on from this, the National Forest School Association is pledged to provide a forum for further research on all areas of Forest School. This began at the 2011 Conference 'Forest School for the 21st Century' where practitioners shared action research and considered ways to bring their case studies and projects to a wider audience. Consulting the association's website will provide links to such new work. My own latest research (Knight, 2011b) explores the perceptions of Forest School embedded in the practices of different Forest School practitioners, and how these indicate that Forest School can be done in many different ways provided that the central ethos remains true.

Discussion points

The data in this chapter may have provoked a range of reactions. Some points you might want to think about are:

- Was there anything that surprised you about the findings above?
- Would replicating the NEF study in more sites be useful?
- What other benefits might you wish to measure?
- How could the outcomes from Forest School be recorded and shared?
- What other recording methods would be useful for Forest School groups?

Further reading

Clark, A. and Moss, P. (2011) *Listening to Young Children: The Mosaic Approach.* 2nd edn. London: National Children's Bureau.

Knight, S. (2011b) Forest School as a way of learning in the outdoors in the UK. *International Journal for Cross-disciplinary Subjects in Education (IJCDSE)*, Special Issue, 1(1).

Leather, M. (2012) 'Seeing the wood from the trees: constructionism and constructivism for outdoor and experiential education', University of Edinburgh. Available at: http://oeandphilosophy2012.newharbour.co.uk/wp-content/uploads/2012/04/Mark-Leather.pdf.

Wattchow, B. and Brown, M. (2011) *A Pedagogy of Space.* Victoria, Australia: Monash University Publishing.

Appendix: Providers of Forest School Training

Training providers in the UK are now appraised by the Forest School Association for the quality of their provision, and prospective students should contact the FSA to check that their chosen trainer is on the up-to-date list of approved training providers. Some of those most likely to be approved are listed below, but this will not be exhaustive, as other providers will come and go. The Forest Education Initiative branches of the Forestry Commission are usually aware of training running in their locations in England, Scotland and Wales. Look on their website, www.foresteducation.org. For the latest UK developments on training and quality assurance issues also check the Institute for Outdoor Education, www.outdoorlearning.org:

Abriachan Forest Trust, Inverness: http://www.abriachan.org.uk/index.htm

Archimedes Training, Sheffield: http://forestschools.com

Big World Adventures, Edinburgh: www.bigworldadventures.org

Birchwood Learning, Norfolk: http://www.birchwoodlearning.com

Bishops Wood Centre, Worcestershire: www.bishopswoodcentre.org.uk

Cambium, Herefordshire: http://www.cambiumsustainable.co.uk/forestschoolstraining.html

Earthcraft, Kent: http://earthcraftuk.com

Forest School Learning Initiative, Gloucestershire: http://www.forestschoollearning.co.uk

Forest School Training Company, Devon: www.forestschooltraining.co.uk

Forest School Wales: http://www.forestschoolwales.org.uk/accessing-forest-school/training-your-own-staff-as-fs-leaders/

Get out of the Classroom, West Midlands: http://getoutoftheclassroom.com

Green Light Trust, Suffolk: http://www.greenlighttrust.org/forest-schools

North Yorkshire Forest School, North Yorks: http://www.forestschooltraining.com

Oxfordshire Forest School: http://www.oxfordshire.gov.uk/cms/content/forest-school

Mindstretchers – Scotland: http://www.mindstretchers.co.uk/contact.cfm

Shropshire Forest School: http://www.shropshire.gov.uk/schools.nsf/open/E800819EC9B43A67802575450054B50C

Staffordshire Wildlife Trust, Staffordshire: http://www.staffs-wildlife.org.uk/page/forest-school-training

Sussex Wildlife Trust: http://www.sussexwildlifetrust.org.uk/education/page00023.htm

Wild Learning, West Midlands: http://wild-learning.com

Glossary

Baden-Powell: Baron Robert Baden-Powell was responsible for the formation of the Boy Scouts through the publication of his book *Scouting for Boys* in 1908, and his sister Agnes for the Girl Guides in 1910. These clubs are still active across the world today, with Beavers and Brownies for younger children, and Rangers for older teenagers.

Children's centres: these are government-funded centres for services to young children and their families, often located with a nursery or school.

Dr Kurt Hahn, 1886–1974: Dr Hahn fled Nazi Germany, giving up the headship of Salem School in southern Germany. He founded Gordonstoun School in Scotland, and also the Outward Bound Movement and others. He identified six declines in modern youth and developed four antidotes, fitness training, expeditions, projects and rescue services. For further details his official website is www. KurtHahn.org.

Early Excellence Centres: the programme to recognise models of good practice in England, Scotland and Wales was set up in 1997.

Early Years Foundation Stage curriculum: the statutory curriculum framework laid down by the UK government for the care and education of children aged 0–5 in day-care settings in England. Published in 2007 and put in place from September 2008, it amalgamates the previous Foundation Stage Curriculum (for 3- to 5-year-olds) with Birth to Three Matters (for 0 to 3-year-olds). It was revised in 2012.

Edexcel: an international examination board based in London. It was formed in 1996 following a merger between BTEC, renowned for its vocational qualifications, and University of London Examinations and Assessment Council, best known for its GCSE and A level examinations.

EYDCP: Early Years Development and Childcare Partnerships were formed in all areas of England and Wales in the late 1990s to bring together representatives of all services for children and their families. In many areas they have now been replaced by other bodies.

Fire pit: an area laid out and assessed as being safe to light a campfire. The ground may or may not be indented, but is not a pit as such, more a defined area.

Forest School: a method of working outdoors with children, young people and adults focusing on their needs and using the natural environment to promote social and emotional progress.

Forest School Leader: someone who has been trained to lead Forest School experiences. They may originally be teachers or environmental leaders or wildlife rangers.

Foundation Stage: in England the Foundation Stage covers children from nought to the beginning of the term after their fifth birthday, when they start compulsory schooling. In Wales the term 'Foundation Phase' includes the first two years of compulsory schooling, extending the upward range to seven, but does not apply until children are three years of age. In Scotland there is a Curriculum Framework for children between the ages of 3 and 5.

Friluftsliv: directly translated as 'open-air life', this term expresses the cultural tradition of spending time in the outdoor environment with family and friends for recreation but also for restoring a personal balance with the aid of nature. Henrik Ibsen first used the term in print in 1859, thus establishing its Norwegian credentials, but the term is common in the other Scandinavian countries. It assumes that every family has easy access to free natural landscapes, and right to roam laws help to preserve this expectation. In Sweden a concern that this tradition is not as strong as it used to be in some areas has led to time being allocated as a part of the national curriculum in schools.

Gordonstoun School: a boarding school situated in Morayshire in Scotland. It is one of 60 schools which are members of the Round Square, an association of schools committed to the educational philosophy of Kurt Hahn. Their philosophy embraces six pillars or precepts which can be summed up in the word IDEALS. They are Internationalism, Democracy, Environment, Adventure, Leadership and Service. In modern times students at Round Square schools make a commitment to addressing each of these pillars through exchanges, work projects, community service and adventure.

Green Light Trust: a charity based in Suffolk with strong links to the hill tribes of Papua New Guinea, committed to bringing communities and landscapes to life through hands-on learning and the growing of woodlands, encouraging each individual to play their role in safeguarding the future.

Higher level teaching assistant (HTLA): non-teaching adults in schools in England and Wales who have undergone training to support teachers with their duties.

In-service training (INSET): a term used to describe the funded training opportunities available to staff working in government-funded schools and nurseries.

Key Stage 1: the National Curriculum in England and Wales is divided into key stages according to the age of the children, and each with its own learning outcomes. Key Stage 1 in England covers the age range from 5 to 7 years.

Local education authorities (LEAs): England is split into authorities responsible, among other things, for distributing and administering aspects of education funding and services.

New Economics Foundation (NEF): an independent organisation which works in partnership with other organisations in a number of ways, including creating strategies for change by developing action research tools.

OCN: The National Open College Network (NOCN) is an awarding body, and organisations such as the Green Light Trust can become accredited OCN centres. This enables them to deliver awards accredited by either NOCN or by one of the regional OCNs. There are 11 OCNs, one in Wales, one in Northern Ireland and one in each of the nine regions of England.

Ofsted: the Office for Standards in Education, Children's Services and Skills is the official body for inspecting schools, nurseries and other childcare providers in England.

Playwork: a description of the profession of workers in out of school settings with children from 4 years to 16 years of age. The sector skills council for Playwork is Skills Active, and accessing their website, www.skillsactive.com/playwork, will enable readers to appreciate the values and assumptions that underpin this profession.

Private, voluntary and independent sector (PVI): this is an expression used to describe day-care and education settings that are not directly funded by the state. It includes childminders, preschools and nurseries.

PSHE: Alongside 'Citizenship', 'Personal, Social and Health Education' is part of the non-statutory framework in the National Curriculum for England and Wales.

Welsh Assembly: the Welsh Assembly government is the devolved government for Wales, and is responsible for most of the day-to-day running of that country.

References and bibliography

Alexander, R. and Hargreaves, L. (2007) *Community Soundings: the Primary Review Regional Witness Sessions*. Cambridge: University of Cambridge Faculty of Education.

Baker, J. (1989) *Where the Forest Meets the Sea*. 2nd edn. London: Walker.

Baldock, P. (2006) *The Place of Narrative in the Early Years Curriculum*. London: Routledge.

Baldock, P., Fitzgerald, D. and Kay, J. (2005) *Understanding Early Years Policy*. London: Paul Chapman.

Barnes, P. and Sharp, B. (eds) (2004) *The RHP Companion to Outdoor Education*. Dorset: Russell House.

Barnes, S. (2007) *How to be Wild*. London: Short Books.

Beaver, M., Brewster, J., Jones, P., Keene, A.L., Neaum, S., Tallack, J., Green, S., Sheppard, H. and Walker, M. (2001) *Babies and Young Children*. Cheltenham: Nelson Thornes.

Becker, P., Schirp, J. and Vollmar, M. (2012) *Abenteuer, Natur und frühe Bildung*. Germany: bsj Jahrbuch.

Bennathan, M. and Boxall, M. (2000) *Effective Intervention in Primary Schools: Nurture Groups*. 2nd edn. London: David Fulton.

Bennett, N., Wood, E. and Rogers, S. (1997) *Teaching through Play*. Buckingham: Open University Press.

Berstrom, M. and Ikonen, P. (2005) 'Space to play, room to grow', *Children in Europe*, 8: 12–13.

Bilton, H. (2003) *Outdoor Play in the Early Years*. 2nd edn. London: David Fulton.

Bilton, H. (2004) *Playing Outside*. London: David Fulton.

Bilton, H., James, K.I., Marsh, J., Wilson, A. and Woonton, M. (2005) *Learning Outdoors*. London: David Fulton.

Black, P., Harrison, C., Lee, C., Marshall, B. and Wiliam, D. (2003) *Assessment for Learning*. Maidenhead: Open University Press.

Blackwell, S. and Pound, L. (2011) 'Forest Schools in the early years', in L. Miller and L. Pound, *Theories and Approaches to Learning in the Early Years*. London: Sage.

BMA (2005) *Preventing Childhood Obesity*. London: BMA Publications.

Bond, S. (2004) 'Forest Schools: a review'. Available at: www.greenlighttrust.org.

Bond, S. (2005) 'Why do Forest Schools'. Available at: www.greenlighttrust.org.

Bond, S. (2007) 'Forest School: relational pedagogy in action'. Available at: www. greenlighttrust.org.

Bonel, P. and Lindon, J. (2000) *Playwork: A Guide to Good Practice*. London: Stanley Thornes.

Borradaile, L. (2006) 'Forest School Scotland: an evaluation'. Available at: www. forestry.gov.uk.

Bratton, C., Crossey, U., Crosby, D. and McKeown, W. (2005) *Learning Outdoors in the Early Years*. Belfast: Early Years Interboard Panel. Available at: http://www.nicurriculum.org.uk/docs/foundation_stage/learning_outdoors.pdf (accessed 3 August 2012).

Brierley, J. (1994) *Give Me a Child Until He is Seven: Brain Studies and Early Childhood Education*. 2nd edn. London: Falmer Press.

Broadhead, P. (2004) *Early Years Play and Learning*. London: RoutledgeFalmer.

Bruce, T. (2004) *Developing Learning in Early Childhood*. London: Paul Chapman.

Bunting, C. (2006) *Interdisciplinary Teaching Through Outdoor Education*. Champaign, IL: Human Kinetics.

BUPA (2007) 'Avoiding childhood obesity'. Available at: http://hcd2.bupa.co.uk/fact_sheets (accessed November 2007).

Burls, A. (2007) 'People and green spaces: promoting public health and mental well-being through ecotherapy', *Journal of Public Mental Health*, 6(3): 24–39.

Butwright, C., Falch-Lovesey, S. and Lord, C. (2007) 'Hopton literacy pilot: using Forest Schools experience as a stimulus for speaking and listening, with a focus on raising achievement in boys' writing using ICT'. Available at: See www.schools.norfolk.gov.uk/myportal/custom.

Callaway, G. (2005) *The Early Years Curriculum: A View from Outdoors*. London: David Fulton.

Carr, M. (2001) *Assessment in Early Childhood Settings*. London: Sage.

Casey, T. (2007) *Environments for Outdoor Play*. London: Paul Chapman.

Cheatum, B. and Hammond, A. (2000) *Physical Activities for Improving Children's Learning and Behaviour*. Champaign, IL: Human Kinetics.

Clark, A. and Moss, P. (2011) *Listening to Young Children*. 2nd edn. London: National Children's Bureau.

Clark, A., McQuail, S. and Moss, P. (2003) *Exploring the Field of Listening to and Consulting with Young Children*. Report RR445. Annesley: DfES.

Claxton, G. (2002) *Building Learning Power*. Bristol: TLO.

Cohen, L., Manion, L. and Morrison, K. (2000) *Research Methods in Education*. 2nd edn. London: RoutledgeFalmer.

Cunningham, H. (2006) *The Invention of Childhood*. London: BBC Books.

Dalberg, G. and Moss, P. (2005) *Ethics and Politics in Early Childhood Education*. London: RoutledgeFarmer.

Davis, B., Rea, T. and Waite, S. (2006) 'The special nature of the outdoors: its contribution to the education of children aged 3–11', *Australian Journal of Outdoor Education*, 10(2): 3–12.

Department for Children, Schools and Families (DCSF) (2005) *Extended Schools: Building on Experience*. London: DCSF.

Department for Children, Schools and Families (DCSF) (2007) 'Government hails "quiet revolution" in school sport'. Available at: www.dfes.gov.uk (accessed November 2007).

Department for Education and Skills (DfES) (2004) *Every Child Matters: Change for Children*. Annesley: DfES Publications.

Department for Education and Skills (DfES) (2007) *The Early Years Foundation Stages*. Annesley: DfES Publications.

Department of Health (DoH) (2000) www.dh.gov.uk/en/Publicationsandstatistics.

Department of Health (DoH) (2004) 'Choosing health', cited in I. Cole-Hamilton (2006), *Play and Health: CPIS Factsheet*. London: Children's Play Council.

Department of Health (DoH) (2005) 'Choosing activity: a physical activity action plan'. Available at: www.dh.gov.uk/en/Publicationsandstatistics (accessed November 2007).

Department of Health (DoH) (2006) *Forecasting Obesity to 2010*. London: Department of Health.

Dowling, M. (2005) *Young Children's Personal, Social and Emotional Development*. 2nd edn. London: Paul Chapman.

Dunn, K., Moore, M. and Murray, P. (2004) *Developing Accessible Play Space: A Good Practice Guide*. London: Office of the Deputy Prime Minister.

Durant, S. (2003) *Outdoor Play*. Leamington Spa: Step Forward.

Economist Intelligence Unit (2012) *Starting Well: Benchmarking Early Education across the World*. London: The Economist.

Education Scotland (2009) *Curriculum for Excellence*. Livingston: Education Scotland. Available at: http://www.educationscotland.gov.uk/Images/all_experiences_outcomes_tcm4-539562.pdf (accessed 3 August 2012).

Edwards, C., Gandini, L. and Forman, G. (eds) (1998) *The Hundred Languages of Children*. London: Ablex.

Farstad, A. (2005) 'Nature: the space provider?', *Children in Europe*, 8: 14–15.

Fisher, J. (1996) *Starting from the Child?* Buckingham: Open University Press.

Gair, N. (1997) *Outdoor Education: Theory and Practice*. London: Cassell.

Garrick, R. (2004) *Playing Outdoors in the Early Years*. London: Continuum.

Gilbertson, K., Bates, T., McLaughlin, T. and Ewert, A. (2006) *Outdoor Education: Methods and Strategies*. Champaign, IL: Human Kinetics.

Gill, T. (2007) *No Fear: Growing Up in a Risk Averse Society*. London: Calouste Gulbenkian Foundation.

Goddard Blythe, S. (2005) *The Well Balanced Child: Movement and Early Learning*. Stroud: Hawthorn Press.

Goodchild, M. (2005) *Ofsted Inspection Report 281747, Nayland Primary School*. London: Ofsted.

Gregory, I. (2003) *Ethics in Research*. London: Continuum.

Gross, R. (1996) *Psychology*. 3rd edn. London: Hodder and Stoughton.

Hannaford, C. (1995) *Smart Moves: Why Learning is Not All in Your Head*. Arlington, VA: Great Ocean.

Health and Social Care Information Centre (2006) BBC news item 'Child obesity doubles in decade'. Available at: www.news.bbc.co.uk/health (accessed November 2007).

Henderson, B. and Vikander, N. (eds) (2007) *Nature First: Outdoor Life the Friluftsliv Way.* Toronto: Natural Heritage Books.

Heywood, C. (2001) *A History of Childhood.* Cambridge: Blackwell.

Higgins, P. and Humberstone, B. (1999) *Outdoor Education and Experiential Learning in the UK.* Germany: Verlag ErlebnispadagogikLuneburg.

Hope, G., Austin, R., Dismore, H., Hammond, S. and Whyte, T. (2007) 'Wild woods or urban jungle: playing it safe or freedom to roam', *Education 3–13,* 35(4): 321–32.

Hopkins, D. and Putnam, R. (1993) *Personal Growth through Adventure.* London: David Fulton.

Howe, A. (2005) *Play Using Natural Materials.* London: David Fulton.

Joyce, R. (2004) 'The Forest Schools of Sweden', *Nursery Education*: December.

Knight, S. (ed.) (2011a) *Forest School for All.* London: Sage.

Knight, S. (2011b) 'Forest School as a way of learning in the outdoors in the UK', *International Journal for Cross-disciplinary Subjects in Education (IJCDSE),* Special Issue, 1(1).

Knight, S. (2011c) *Risk and Adventure in Early Years Outdoor Play.* London: Sage.

Knight, S. (ed.) (2013) *International Perspectives on Forest School.* London: Sage.

Kraftl, P., Horton, J. and Tucker, F. (2012) *Critical Geographies of Childhood and Youth.* Bristol: Policy Press.

Kubala, P. (2002) *Friluftsliv – the Mysterious, the Ordinary, the Noticeable, and the Extraordinary.* Olomouc, Czech Republic: Palacky University.

Learning Through Landscapes, 'The value of outdoor play'. Available at: www.ltl. org. uk/school_and_settings (accessed 2006).

Leather, M. (2012) 'Seeing the wood from the trees: constructionism and constructivism for outdoor and experiential education', University of Edinburgh. Available at: http://oeandphilosophy2012.newharbour.co.uk/wp-content/uploads/2012/04/Mark-Leather.pdf

Lechte, J. (1994) *Fifty Key Contemporary Thinkers.* London: Routledge

Lindon, J. (2001) *Understanding Children's Play.* Cheltenham: Nelson Thornes.

Lindon, J. (2003) *Too Safe for Their Own Good?* London: National Children's Bureau.

Lindon, J. (2011) *Too Safe for Their Own Good?* 2nd edn. London: National Children's Bureau.

Litchman, M. (2006) *Qualitative Research in Education: A User's Guide.* London: Sage.

Little, H. (2006) 'Children's risk-taking behaviour: implications for early childhood policy and practice', *International Journal of Early Years Education,* 14(2): 141–54.

Louv, R. (2005) *Last Child in the Woods: Saving Our Children from Nature-Deficit Disorder.* London: Atlantic Books.

Louv, R. (2010) *Last Child in the Woods: Saving Our Children from Nature-Deficit Disorder.* 2nd edn. London: Atlantic Books.

Lovell, R. (2008) 'Physical activity at Forest School', Forestry Commission Scotland. Available at: www.forestry.gov.uk/centralscotland.

Macintyre, C. and McVitty, K. (2004) *Movement and Learning in the Early Years*. London: Paul Chapman.

MacNaughton, G., Rolfe, S. and Siraj-Blatchford, I. (2001) *Doing Early Childhood Research*. Buckingham: Open University Press.

Martin, A., Franc, D. and Zounkova, D. (2004) *Outdoor and Experiential Learning*. Aldershot: Gower.

Maslow, A. (1954) *Motivation and Personality*. New York: Harper & Row.

Maude, P. (2001) *Physical Children, Active Teaching*. Buckingham: Open University Press.

Maynard, T. (2007a) 'Forest Schools in Great Britain: an initial exploration', *Contemporary Issues in Early Childhood*, 8(4): 320–31.

Maynard, T. (2007b) 'Encounters with Forest School and Foucault: a risky business?', *Education 3–13*, 35(4): 379–91.

Montessori Education UK, www.montessorieducationuk.org.

Morrow, V. (2010) 'Children's "social capital"', in J. Rix, M. Nind, K. Sheehy, K. Simmons and C. Walsh (eds) (2010) *Equality, Participation and Inclusion*. 2nd edn. Abingdon: Routledge.

Mortlock, C. (2000) *The Adventure Alternative*. Cumbria: Cicerone Press.

Moser, T. and Martinsen, M. (2010) 'The outdoor environment in Norwegian kindergartens as pedagogical space for toddlers' play, learning and development', paper given at 20th EECERA Conference, Birmingham.

Moss, B. (2009) 'Ethics, vision and values: the challenge of spirituality', in J. McKimm and K. Phillips (eds), *Leadership and Management in Integrated Services*. Exeter: Learning Matters.

Murray, R. (2004) *Forest School Evaluation Project: A Study in Wales*. Report carried out by New Economics Foundation (NEF). Available at: www.neweconomics.com.

Murray, R. and O'Brien, L. (2005) *Such Enthusiasm – a Joy to See: An Evaluation of Forest School in England*. Report carried out by New Economics Foundation (NEF). Available at: www.neweconomics.org.

National Audit Office (2006) 'Tackling child obesity – first steps'. Available at: www. nao.org.uk/publications/nao_reports/0506.

Natural England (2009) 'Childhood and nature: a survey on changing relationships with nature across generations'. Available at: http://www.naturalengland.org. uk/Images/Childhood%20and%20Nature%20Survey_tcm6-10515.pdf.

New Zealand Ministry of Education (1996) *Te Whariki: Early Childhood Curriculum*. Wellington, NZ: Learning Media.

Nicol, J. (2007) *Bringing the Steiner Waldorf Approach to Your Early Years Practice*. London: David Fulton.

Nilsson, K., Sangster, M., Gallis, C., Hartig, T., de Vries, S., Seeland, K. and Schipperijn, J. (eds) (2012) *Forests, Trees and Human Health*. New York: Springer Books.

O'Brien, L. and Murray, R. (2006) *A Marvellous Opportunity for Children to Learn*. Report carried out by the Forestry Commission and New Economics Foundation (NEF). Available at: www.neweconomics.org.

O'Brien, L. and Murray, R. (2007) 'Forest School and its impacts on young children: case studies in Britain', *Urban Forestry and Urban Greening*, 6: 249–65. Available at: http://www.forestry.gov.uk/fr/infd-5z3jvz.

O'Brien, L. and Tabbush, P. (2002) *Health and Well-being: Trees, Woodlands and Natural Spaces*. Edinburgh: Forestry Commission.

Oldfield, L. (2001) *Free to Learn*. Stroud: Hawthorn Press.

Palmer, S. (2006) *Toxic Childhood*. London: Orion.

Peacock, J., Hine, R. and Pretty, J. (2007) *Ecotherapy Report*. London: MIND. Available at: http://www.mind.org.uk/campaigns_and_issues/report_and_resources/835_ecotherapy

Pugh, G. (1996) *Contemporary Issues in the Early Years*. London: Paul Chapman.

QCA (2006) *Learning Outside: the Classroom Manifesto*. London: DfES Publications.

Raphael Steiner School prospectus. Available at: www.raphaelsteinerschool.co.uk.

Reggio Emilia, www.zerosei.commune.re.it.

Render, M. (2003) *Woodland for Life: The Regional Woodland Strategy for the East of England*. London: EEDA and Forestry Commission.

Rickinson, M., Dillon, J., Teamey, K., Morris, M., Choi, M., Sanders, D. and Benefield, P. (2004) *A Review of Research on Outdoor Learning*. London: NFER and King's College.

Riggall, A. and Sharp, C. (2008) 'The structure and content of English primary education: international perspectives', *Primary Review*, 8, (February). Available at: www.primaryreview.org.uk.

Roberts, R. (2006) *Self-Esteem and Early Learning*. London: Paul Chapman.

Robinson, G. (1995) *Sketch-books: Explore and Store*. London: Hodder and Stoughton.

Robinson, T. (2001) *Out of Our Minds: Learning to be Creative*. Chichester: Capstone.

Robinson, T. (2006) 'Out of our minds: learning to be creative'. Available at: www.ted.com/index.php/talks/view/id/66.

Robson, C. (2002) *Real World Research*. 2nd edn. Oxford: Blackwell.

Rodger, R. (2003) *Planning an Appropriate Curriculum for the Under Fives*. 2nd edn. London: David Fulton.

Roe, J., Aspinall, P. and Ward Thompson, C. (2008) 'Forest School: evidence for restorative health benefits in young people', Forestry Commission Scotland. Available at: www.forestry.gov.uk/centralscotland.

Ryder Richardson, G. (2006) *Creating a Space to Grow*. London: David Fulton.

Sandell, K. (1993) 'Outdoor recreation and the Nordic tradition of "Friluftsliv": a source of inspiration for a sustainable society?', *Trumpeter*, 10:1. Available at: www.icaap.org.

Sheridan, M., Cockerill, H. and Sharma, A. (2007) *From Birth to Five Years: Children's Developmental Progress*. 2nd edn. London: Routledge.

Silverman, D. (2005) *Doing Qualitative Research*. London: Sage.

Taylor, S. (2005) 'Norway', *Early Years Educator*, 7(6): 68–71.

Tovey, H. (2007) *Playing Outdoors, Spaces and Places, Risk and Challenge*. Maidenhead: Open University Press.

Training and Development Agency for Schools (2006) 'Extended schools programme.' Available at: www.tda.gov.uk.

Trout, M. (2004) 'All about Forest Schools', *Nursery World*, Supplement: 15–22.

Waine, C. (2006) BBC news item 'Child obesity doubles in decade'. Available at: www.news.bbc.co.uk/health (accessed November 2007).

Waite, S. (ed.) (2011) *Children Learning Outside the Classroom*, London: Sage.

Waite, S. and Pratt, N. (2012) 'School gardens: teaching and learning outside the front door', *Education 3–13: International Journal of Primary, Elementary and Early Years Education*, 17 February.

Waller, T. (2006) 'Don't come too close to my octopus tree: recording and evaluating young children's perspectives on outdoor environments', *Children, Youth and Environments*, 16(2): 75–104.

Waller, T. (2007) 'The trampoline tree and the swamp monster with 18 heads: outdoor play in the Foundation Stage and Foundation Phase', *Education 3–13*, 35(4): 393–407.

Walsh, M. (2001) *Research Made Real*. Cheltenham: Nelson Thornes.

Warden, C. (2005) *The Potential of a Puddle*. Perthshire: Mindstretchers.

Waters, J. and Begley, S. (2007) 'Supporting the development of risk-taking behaviours in the early years: an exploratory study', *Education 3–13*, 35(4): 365–77.

Wattchow, B. and Brown, M. (2011) *A Pedagogy of Space*. Victoria, Australia: Monash University Publishing.

Wellings, E. (2012) *Forest School National Governing Body Business Plan 2012*. Carlisle: Institute for Outdoor Learning, p.8, available at: www.outdoor-learning.org

Welsh Assembly (2008), *Framework for Children's Learning for 3- to 7-year-olds in Wales*. Cardiff: Welsh Assembly Government. Available at: http://wales.gov.uk/dcells/publications/policy_strategy_and_planning/early-wales/whatisfoundation/foundationphase/2274085/frameworkforchildrene.pdf?lang=en (accessed 3 August 2012).

Weston, P. (2000) *Friedrich Froebel: His Life, Times and Significance*. 2nd edn. London: Roehampton Institute.

Williams-Siegfredsen, J. (2005) 'Run the risk', *Nursery World*, August: 26–7.

Wood, E. and Attfield, J. (2005) *Play, Learning and the Early Childhood Curriculum*. 2nd edn. London: Paul Chapman.

Yelland, N. (2005) *Critical Issues in Early Childhood Education*. Maidenhead: Open University Press.

Index

Added to a page number 'f' denotes a figure, 't' denotes a table and 'g' denotes glossary.

ability 78
accidents 39
active learning 58
activities
  carefully-planned 36
  Forest School
    adult-led 98
    child-led/initiated 45, 78
    development, Northern Europe 4
    examples 79–80t
    ideal site for 69–71
    in other settings 101–5
    risk assessment 75f
  increase in family 37
  outdoor 39
  self-regulated 37
addict group (Phoenix Futures) 48, 50, 51, 53
adult attitudes 91
adult intervention 86
adult participation 98
adult-child ratios 73
adventure 39, 70
adventure playgrounds 40–1, 102
adventurous spirit 40, 41

after-school clubs 36
agency 51, 53, 138
All Saints School, Lawshall 25–8, 119
    longitudinal study 129–37
Anglia Ruskin University 10
antisocial behaviour 39, 45
aptitudes 62
artwork 85
Assessment in Early Childhood Settings 61
attachment 43
attention deficit hyperactivity disorder (ADHD) 42
attitudes 6, 35, 40, 43, 91, 102, 138
auditory exploration 80f
Australia 116
autonomy 51, 78
awareness-raising sessions 103
awe and wonder 58, 125

babies 43, 44, 70, 71, 91
Baden-Powell movement 3, 142g
balancing 37
Barnes, Simon 53, 54
base camps 70, 71, 81

Becker, P. 138
beginning sessions 20, 24, 28, 30, 32
behaviour 37–42, 43, 44, 45
    see also emotional and behavioural difficulties
behaviour problems 35, 42
beliefs 44
belonging 45, 61
Bilton, H. 85, 134
Bishops Wood Centre 10, 11–13
blocks of sessions 19, 20, 23, 24, 26, 28, 29, 30, 31, 32
    six week example 73–86
BMA report (2005) 35
boats 102–3
body dissatisfaction 35
børnehaven 5, 6–7
boundaries 44, 45, 81, 94
boys 3, 38, 42, 82–3, 98
Brady, Mike 48
brain 4, 19
Bridgwater College 106–7, 108
    development of Forest School 5–6
    expansion of Forest School idea 8–13
    trip to Denmark 4–5
Broadhead, Pat 20
Bronfenbrenner, U. 44
Brown, M. 138
brushwood 70
Building Learning Power 57, 61–2
BUPA (2007) 35
Burls, A. 49
Burnworthy Outdoor Education Centre 8, 106–7
    Women's refuge group 47, 50, 51, 53
Burrows, Kevin 115

Carr, Margaret 61
central glades 71
challenge 19, 20, 39, 41, 60
child well-being 38, 42, 116, 138
child-centredness 59, 62, 63, 64
child-led/initiated
    learning and development 63, 125
    play/activities 7, 45, 57, 78
childcare 45
childhood 38
Children and Nature movement 116

Children's Centre group 48, 50, 51, 53
children's centres 142g
A Child's Christmas in Wales 39
choice 35, 41
Clark, A. 65
Claxton, Guy 57, 61–2, 63
closure sessions 80f
clothing 5, 6, 23, 26–7, 29, 31, 79–81, 102
collaboration 62
communication 52–3, 115
    see also dialogue(s); language and communication
community 44–5, 59, 61
community involvement 111
compulsory education 4
concentration 42, 45, 49, 85, 107, 125
confidence 43, 45, 48, 50, 51, 68, 69, 70, 78, 87, 107, 108, 124
consistency 43, 44
continuing professional development 100, 104
control 83
cooking 97
cooperation 60, 62, 68, 78, 86, 87, 102, 108, 115
cooperative play 20
coping mechanisms 50
coppicing, wood for 69
county councils 10, 28, 30
creative play 98
creativity 6, 58, 59, 63, 64, 92, 115
criminalisation of play 38
critical thinking 63
culture 44
Cunningham, Hugh 38
curiosity 62, 125
curriculum
    Early Years Foundation Stage 8, 57, 63, 90–1, 97–8, 142–3g
    Foundation Phase (Wales) 73, 81
    suppression of creativity 63
    see also hidden curriculum; National Curriculum
Curriculum for Excellence 68, 78

daily site check, risk assessment 76f
Danish Garden 12–13

Daws Hall Centre 28
day-care settings 43
decision-making 41, 68, 78, 83, 84,
    86, 87, 108
deep forest 70
deep play 19, 93, 98
Denmark 4–5, 6–7, 40
dens 40, 93
Department for Children, Schools
    and Families (DCSF) 13, 35
Department of Health 13, 35
depression 35
desensitisation 94
dialogue(s) 59, 66
Dilham Preschool 109
discrimination 35
discussion 66
dispositions 43
diversity 73

Early Excellence Centres 6,
    11, 142g
Early Years Development and
    Childcare Partnerships (EYDCP)
    11, 143g
Early Years Foundation Stage (EYFS)
    8, 57, 63, 90–1, 97–8, 142–3g
Early Years Interboard Panel
    (Northern Ireland) 73
Economist Intelligence Unit 57
Edexcel 8, 143g
education 2, 4, 6, 10, 63
Education Act (1944) 4
Education Select Committee
    (2005) 37
educational outcomes 138
elder (wood) 69, 71
emotional and behavioural
    difficulties
  assessment 77f
  Forest School for 111–12
emotional environment 70
emotional stability 6
empathy 60, 98
empowerment 52, 53, 61
Entry to Employment scheme
    (YMCA) 114
environment
  access to 6
  contact with 95
  control of 83
  engagement with 6–8, 37

environment *cont.*
  ideal 70
  respect for 5, 18
  safe 18–19, 22–3, 25–6, 29, 31, 72
  see also learning environments;
      natural environment; outdoor
      environment
environmental awareness 78
environmental centre, Bishops Wood
    10, 11–13
environmental psychology 42
episodic memory 83
equipment 59, 102–3
Essex County Council 10, 28
Essex Wildlife Trust 111–12
ethos 8, 16, 58, 65, 66, 92
Europe 4
events 64
Every Child Matters (2004) 5
example 58
excitement 19, 39
excluded pupils, programme for
    112–14
exercise 3, 35, 36, 37, 41
experience 64
exploration 70, 80f, 81, 92, 125
extreme challenge 60

Falch-Lovesey, Sue 30
family engagement 48
fibreglass 102–3
final sessions 20, 24, 28, 30, 32
fire pits 71, 97, 143g
fires 6, 97
Fisher, J. 84
flexibility 37, 82
Forest Education Initiative (FEI) 9,
    10, 103
  see also NEF/FEI studies
Forest School for the 21st Century
    (2011) 139
Forest School(s)
  access to 89
  in action (examples) 108–15
  activities *see* activities; play
  benefits 73, 85, 107–8
  as a counter to obesity 35–7
  definition 16, 143g
  description 18–21
  differing beliefs about 16
  effect on behaviour 37–42
  ethos 8, 16, 58, 65, 66, 92

Forest School(s) *cont.*
  expansion of the Bridgwater idea
    8–13
  external influences on 56–66
  from Scandinavia to Somerset
    4–8
  historical roots in the UK 2–4
  impact on social development
    42–5
  international developments
    115–16
  leaders 9, 19, 53, 100, 143g
  long-term effects 54
  looking forward 13–14
  outcomes research 118–39
  principles for good practice 17–18
  site selection 68–71
  testing the definition of (examples)
    21–32
  typical block of sessions 73–86
  see also individual schools
Forest School for All 2, 45, 48
Forest School Association (FSA) 11,
  13, 117, 138, 139
*Forest School Evaluation Project: A
  Study in Wales* 9, 119
Forest School GB Trainers
  Network 16
Forest School NGB Working
  Group 16
Forest Schools, benefits 21
Forestry Commission 8–9, 40, 41, 68,
  71, 138
Foundation Phase 73, 81, 143g
Foundation Stage 9, 21, 42,
  119, 143g
Framlingham Early School 114
free play 6, 90
freedom 38
friluftsliv 5, 143g
Frithy Wood 25–8, 112–14
Froebel, F. 3, 6, 57–8
funding 36, 100, 103, 109, 110, 111

games (safety) 81
gardening tools 103
gardens 42, 93
Garrick, R. 83
generative thinking 63
geographical space 138
Germany 58, 116
Gibson, Becky 111

Gill, Tim 38
girls 3, 98
Gordonstoun School 3, 144g
government reports 13
Green Light Trust 10, 21, 144g
  Project 112–14
group base, distance of site from 71
group decisions 83
'guardians of the forest' 27

habits 10, 35, 37
Hahn, Dr Kurt 3, 142
Hall, Diane 109–10
Hanningfield Reservoir Nature
  Reserve 111–12
hazards 39, 40, 60, 72
hazel 69, 71
health 49
health and safety 4, 38, 61
Health and Safety Executive 72
heuristic play 95
hidden curriculum 91
hierarchy of needs (Maslow's) 4
higher-level teaching assistants
  (HLTA) 144g
holistic development 61
Hopkins, Fi 45
Houghton Hall 30–2
How to be Wild 53

Ibsen, Henrik 143
ICT 38, 65
ideal sites 69–71
ideas 64
imagination 62
imaginative play 69
imitation 58
in-service training (INSET) 31,
  103, 144g
independence 38, 83
individuality 59
induction sessions, for parents 104
industrialisation 2–3
insecurity 43
'instinct for adventure' 39
Institute for Outdoor Education 11,
  13, 16, 24, 60
intelligence 64
international developments 107,
  115–16
*International Perspectives on Forest
  School* 116

introductory presentation, for
   parents 73
intuitive skills 24–5
investigation 71
Isaacs, Susan 3, 20
ivy, trails of 70–1

John Bunyan Infant School 28–30,
   48, 50, 53

Kenninghall Primary School 111
Key Stage 1 144g
key workers 52
kindergarten 5, 58
knowledge 49, 53–4, 108, 125–6, 137
Korea 116
Kraftl, P. 138

landscaping 97
language and communication 49,
   107, 124–5, 137
leaders 9, 19, 53, 100, 143g
learning 43, 59, 64
   active, open-ended 58
   child-initiated 63, 125
   place and 53–4
   tailoring 66
   see also play-based learning; rich
      learning; social learning
learning environments 91
learning stories 61, 65
learning styles 134
Leather, Mark 138
Lechte, J. 51
legislation, fear of 39
leisure time 41
Level 1 Forest Skills 24, 100
Level 3 Forest Skills 8, 69, 71, 72, 100
levels, creating different 96–7
light 70
Lindon, Jenny 38
Lings Wood 109–10
listening 59, 63
literacy work 65
local education authorities 144g
long-term effects
   study 129–37
   working with adults 54
Louv, Richard 36, 38, 54, 91, 116

McMillan, Margaret and Rachel 3
magic atmospheres/places 92, 94

magic carpets 93–4
make-believe 58
Malaguzzi, Loris 59
map sticks 81
marshmallow toasting 86
A Marvellous Opportunity for Children
   to Learn 9
Maslow's hierarchy of needs 4
media reports, bad behaviour 38
mental health charities 49
Mind 49
Mindstretchers 102
minibeasts 70, 96–7
mobility 96
moderate learning difficulties, Forest
   School for 111–12, 115
monoculture 71
Montessori, M. 57, 58–9
Mortlock, Colin 39, 60, 94
motivation 42, 43, 45, 49, 68, 87,
   107, 108, 125
mouth objects 95
Muddypuddles 102
Murray, Richard 107, 120, 121,
   129, 138
myelinisation 19

National Curriculum 38, 125
National Occupational Standards 13
National Open College Network
   (NOCN) 144
National Trust 40, 41, 71
Natural England 40
natural environment 3, 9, 41,
   50, 62
natural materials 58, 59, 63, 93, 98
natural objects 95
natural spaces 100
naturbørnehaven 5, 7–8
nature
   contact/connection with 42, 49,
      50, 53
   respect for 60
Nature Kindergarten 5
nature reserves 109–10, 111–12
Nayland School 13, 22–5
   longitudinal study 129–30
   questionnaire 130–3
   results 134–7
   self-appraisal study 118–19
   comparison with NEF/FEI studies
      128–9

Nayland School *cont.*
   discussion on identified
      outcomes 124–6
   recording sessions 126–7
   reflection poster 127–8
   storyboarding exercise 121–4
needs, hierarchy of 4
NEF/FEI studies 9, 37, 48, 118,
   119–20
   replication at Nayland *see* Nayland
     School
negative feedback 43
negotiation 86, 98
neural pathways 19
New Economics Foundation
   (NEF) 144g
   see also NEF/FEI studies
new perspectives 108, 126
New Zealand 60–1, 65
noises, experiment with 84–5
Norfolk Broads Authority 114
Norfolk Country Council 10, 30
Northern Ireland 73, 83
Norway 5
NR5 Project 114
numerical guide, to risk 72

obesity 35–7
O'Brien, Liz 107, 120, 121,
   129, 138
observation(s) 59, 65
Ofsted 13, 145g
older children 44, 92
'1, 2, 3' safety game 81
Open College Network (OCN) 8, 9,
   10, 144g
open-ended play 20
organised exercise 41
outdoor activities 39
Outdoor Adventure Education 60
outdoor education 138
outdoor environment 2, 3,
   57, 91
outdoor play 35, 57, 59, 90–101
Outward Bound movement 3
ownership 78, 100, 126, 138
Oxfordshire County Council 10

Palmer, Sue 41–2
parental attitudes 40
parental fears 36
parental involvement 59

parents
   induction sessions for 104
   introductory presentations for 73
   working with 47–54, 111
Parkhall Wood 28–30
partnership 50, 73, 109–10
Partridge, Lucy 48, 50
pedagogy 10, 63, 138
permanent change 19
personal development 59
Pestalozzi, J.H. 3, 57, 58
Philosophical Perspectives in
   Outdoor Education 138
Phoenix Futures group 48, 50,
   51, 53
physical education 4, 35–6
physical skills 37, 49, 69, 108, 125
place, as a learning context
   53–4
planning 78, 91
plants 71
play
   child-led 7, 57
   creative 98
   criminalisation of 38
   imaginative 69
   importance in development 3
   open-ended 20
   solitary 98
   spontaneous 45
   undirected 83
   unseen 93
   see also deep play; free play;
     outdoor play; role play
Play Safety Forum 40
play-based learning 20, 23–4, 27–8,
   29, 31–2, 97–100
playgrounds 38, 40
playing fields 4, 40
playtimes 4
Playwork 92, 145g
positive partnerships 73
possibles 59
post-feminism 51
post-modernism 63
post-structuralism 63
potato peelers, using 85
pram insulation 91
Pratt, N. 53
precautionary approach, to public
   settings 38
Preventing Childhood Obesity 35

private, voluntary and independent
    sector (PVI) 145g
progress, risk and 40
PSHE 145g
psychological consequences,
    obesity 35
psychological well-being 42
public access, on sites 71
public attitudes 40
public spaces/settings 38, 39, 40
Putnam, Roger 40

Quality Assurance schemes 24
quality of care 45

Raindrops 102
reciprocity 51, 62
Reclaiming Relational Pedagogy in
    the Early Years 10
recording/systems 59, 61, 65
reflection 65
reflective diaries 27
reflective practitioners 62, 65–6
Reggio Emilia approach 59, 61,
    63, 98
relationships 21, 43, 48, 50, 51,
    61, 137
repetition 19, 58–9
resilience 37, 42, 62
resourcefulness 53, 62
respect 44, 52
responsibility 38, 53
rich learning 83
Rigby, Sally 111
ripple effects 108, 126, 137
risk(s) 37, 39, 40, 41, 116
risk assessment 19, 60, 72–3,
    74–7f, 78
risk management 71
risk-averse society 38, 41
risk-taking 6, 18–19, 40, 58, 60, 81,
    94–7
roads, security from 71
Robinson, Gill 65
Robinson, Ken 63, 64
role play 85–6
rotting wood 70
rules 18, 38, 45, 98

safe areas 82
safe environments 18–19, 22–3, 25–6,
    29, 31, 72

safety 36, 40, 78, 81, 94, 97
    see also accidents; health and
        safety; security
Sangtae Kindergarten 116
scaffolding 66
Scandinavia 4–5, 6, 58
school leaving age 4
school-based activities 79f
scientific discovery 95
Scotland 9–10, 68, 78, 118,
    138, 143
scrapbooks 65
screening 93
seasonal site, risk assessment 74f
secret atmospheres/places 92,
    93, 94
secure attachment 43
secure base 44
security 43, 45, 71, 81
SEEVIC College 114–15
Self-Appraisal Toolkit 120
    use at Nayland see Nayland School
self-awareness 62, 78
self-belief 51
self-care 44
self-concept 60
self-control 44
self-discipline 62
self-esteem 35, 43, 45, 50, 51, 60, 68,
    87, 108
self-help 44, 45
self-image 44
self-regulated activities 37
self-respect 52
sense of community 44–5
sensitivity 94, 98
sensory awareness 78, 80f
sensory experiences 58
sensory play 59
separateness 92, 94
sessions 20, 24, 28, 30, 32
    see also blocks of sessions
settings
    Forest School 18, 22, 25, 28, 30–1,
        92–4
    Forest School-type activities in
        other 101–5
shade 93
shared storytelling 100
sharp tools 103
sheds 92–3
Shellabear, Jane 110

siblings, separation from 43
singing 82
sisterhood 51
sites
  ownership of 78, 100
  risk assessment 74f, 76f, 78
  selection 68–71
sketchbooks 65
Sketchbooks: Explore and Store 65
skills 53–4, 62, 86–7, 126
  see also physical skills; social skills
'Skills for Life' agenda 107–8
skogsbørnehaven 5
skogsmulle 5
smell and feel exploration 80f
social capital 51–2
social constructivism 138
social development 42–5
Social and Economic Research Group
  of Forest Research 9
Social and Emotional Aspects of
  Learning (SEAL) 27
social geography 138
social interaction(s) 20, 53, 58
social learning 86
social pedagogy 138
social rules 98
social skills 42, 45, 48, 107, 124
socialisation 6
solitary play 98
sound/noise 84–5
soup 97
space
  for exploration and adventure 70
  increasing the amount of 96
  sense of 138
  see also natural spaces; public
    spaces
Special Interest Group 13, 16, 60
spirituality 52
sponsorship 103
spontaneous play 45
sport 35–6
staffing issues 103–4
  see also training
stag beetles 70
standards 13
Steiner Waldorf approach 57,
  58, 98
sticks 82
storage areas 12f, 102
storm damage 86

storytelling, shared 100
Strategic Planning for Children's
  Centres 48
strength 37
*Such Enthusiasm – a Joy to See; an
  Evaluation of Forest School in
  England* 9
Sure Start *see* Children's Centre group
surfaces 95
sustainable development 116
Sweden 5, 143
symbolic thought 64

task ownership 78
Taylor, Wendy 48, 50
Te Whariki 60–1, 63
teamwork 108
Texas A & M University 42
therapeutic gardens 42
Thomas, Dylan 39
tools 85, 103
Toxic Childhood 41–2
trails of ivy 70–1
training 13, 20, 24, 28, 30, 31, 32,
  72, 97, 100, 103, 144
training providers 140–1
transporting objects 95
travel 71
tree trunks 69
trees 9, 40, 71, 92, 97
trust 20, 23, 27, 29, 31, 93

understanding 49, 53–4, 63, 108,
  125–6, 137
undirected play 83
UNICEF (2007) 38
United States 42, 116
University of Minnesota 42

values 73
visual exploration 80f
Vocational Inclusion Programme 12
vulnerable adults, working
  with 49

Waite, S. 53
waiting trees 29
Wales 9, 73, 81, 138, 143
Waller, Tim 138
Wandekinder 116
water 95, 97
Wattchow, B. 138

weather 5, 19, 23, 26–7, 79, 86
weatherproof suits 102
well-being 38, 42, 116, 138
Wellings, Erica 16
Welsh Assembly 9, 145g
wheelchair users 96
Where the Forest Meets the Sea 86
wild world, engagement with 53
wildlife trusts 10, 109,
    111–12
willow 69
Wilson, Russell 114
women, as a sisterhood 51

Women's Refuge group (Burnworthy)
    47, 50, 51, 53
wood 69, 70, 85
wood-based activities 79f
woodland 5, 9, 70
Woodland for Life 9
Woodland policy 10
woodworking tools 103
woven mat 61
wrap-around care 92

YMCA Entry to Employment
    scheme 114